SEWING for SUMMER

Simple projects for the
perfect summer wardrobe

Kristy Chan

NEW
HOLLAND

Published in 2015 by
New Holland Publishers
London • Sydney • Auckland

The Chandlery Unit 9 50 Westminster Bridge Road London SE1 7QY United Kingdom
1/66 Gibbes Street Chatswood NSW 2067 Australia
5/39 Woodside Ave Northcote, Auckland 0627 New Zealand

www.newhollandpublishers.com

A catalogue record of this book is available at the British Library and the National Library of Australia.

ISBN: 9781742575667

Managing Director: Fiona Schultz
Publisher: Diane Ward
Project Editor: Holly Willsher
Design: Andrew Quinlan
Cover Design: Lorena Susak
Production Director: Olga Dementiev
Printer: Toppan Leefung Printing Ltd (China)
Photographer: Samantha Mackie

10 9 8 7 6 5 4 3 2 1

Follow New Holland Publishers on
Facebook: www.facebook.com/NewHollandPublishers

Contents

Introduction

There has never been a better time to learn to sew your own clothes – for a long time sewing was considered a hobby that only our grandmothers had the time or need to do, but now people of all ages are discovering the fun and satisfaction of making their own clothes and accessories. Fantastic fabrics are available in a huge variety of colours and prints from fabric stores and on-line sellers, and there is just so much inspiration thanks to blogs, Pinterest and Instagram.

By sewing your own clothes not only will they fit you exactly the way you want them to, but best of all you can make them in whatever colour and print you choose. And this means that you'll never see someone else wearing the same outfit as you! Sewing can save you money, especially if you use thrift store fabrics or upcycle other fabrics for reuse such as vintage sheets, table cloths or old clothes and the like.

In this book you will find instructions and patterns for 25 simple projects that will make an entire summer wardrobe. There are fabric covered beads for days when it's just too hot for jewellery, cover ups and sarongs for days at the beach, simple skirts and tops to help cope with the hot days and loose pants and a kimono jacket for those cooler summer evenings. There are also instructions to make a big beach tote bag to carry all your necessary things, as well as a smaller shoulder bag for fun nights out.

Your sewing machine manual will show you how to thread your sewing machine and how to do basic stitches. The techniques chapter in this book will build on those basic skills by explaining some techniques that are very useful for making clothes that look great and that you will be proud to tell everyone that you made it yourself!

Tools and Techniques

TOOLS

You could sew all the projects in this book by hand with nothing more than a needle and thread, but that would take a long time and the stitching wouldn't be as neat as machine stitching. The following equipment is very useful for making your own clothes:

Sewing machine: you don't need a brand new or really expensive sewing machine with lots of fancy stitches when you're starting out learning to sew. A sewing machine that will do a straight stitch and a zig zag stitch is all you really need, although a machine that does a one-step buttonhole will make it much easier when you're ready to start making buttonholes in your clothes.

Overlocker: also known as a serger, an overlocker neatens the raw edges of fabrics and stops fabric fraying by cutting and wrapping the edge in stitching. An overlocker can also be used as a quick way to sew knit fabrics instead of a sewing machine. This is an expensive machine and isn't really necessary as there are other ways to neaten the raw edges of fabric (see the techniques described page 11–13), however an overlocker is very useful for more advanced sewing projects.

Scissors: the cardinal rule for sewing scissors is to use them only on fabric and never use them to cut paper. Paper will blunt the blades very quickly and they won't be able to cut through fabric. A pair of dressmaking shears is essential for cutting out fabrics. Other useful scissors include smaller sharp scissors for detailed work such as snipping seam allowances or cutting in small spaces, such as cutting open buttonholes and thread snips for snipping off threads. Pinking shears are also very useful (scissors with a zig-zag shaped cutting blade) for cutting the edges of fabric to reduce fraying.

Seam ripper/unpicker: an unpicker is used for picking out stitches when you've made a mistake. In an ideal world you wouldn't need one, but the reality is you'll probably use one frequently – we all make mistakes!

Pins: they come in a variety of different types, such as fine pins for delicate fabrics, thick pins for heavy fabrics and universal pins that suit most fabrics. Glass head beads are a good option because they are easy to handle and are visible on the fabric and on the floor if you drop them. Remember that pins can get blunt after they've been used for a while, when they are hard to push into the fabric throw them in the bin and buy some new ones.

Measuring tape: essential for getting accurate measurements of your body so that you can pick the right size sewing pattern. A measuring tape is also used for working out hem lengths.

Machine needles: your sewing machine will need different needles depending on the fabric you are sewing. Universal needles work well on woven fabrics, but to sew a stretchy fabric you'll need to put stretch or ball point needles in your sewing machine. For heavier fabrics or leather, you'll need jeans or leather machine needles.

Hand sewing needles: even if you do most of your sewing using your sewing machine, there will still be times that you'll need to do some hand sewing, such as sewing on buttons or press studs. A pack of hand sewing needles of various sizes will be all you need for clothes sewing.

Threads: threads come in a variety of fibre contents for different purposes. For sewing clothes, polyester thread is the best.

Elastic: elastic comes in a lot of different widths and types, but for the projects in this book a woven or non-roll elastic will be best in a width of approximately 25mm/1in unless you prefer a wider waistband. You can also find elastic in different colours, which can look very fun when used as an exposed waistband.

Press studs: press studs are used as an alternative to buttons to do up clothing. They are two small discs that are hand sewn to the fabric at the point where they need to join.

Fabric: if you have been in any fabric store you will know that there is a huge variety of fabrics. For clothes making, there are two main types of fabric: knit and woven.

Knit fabrics are those fabrics where the fibres have been knitted together and because of this knit fabrics are stretchy. The amount of stretch will vary depending on the type of knit fabric – from cotton interlock with little stretch used for t-shirts to polyester lycra used for swimwear and everything in between. The great things about knit fabrics is that they are quick to sew as the edges won't unravel, they are forgiving to fit because of their stretch and best of all they don't wrinkle easily. Knit fabrics also come in a great range of colours and prints.

Woven fabrics are those fabrics where the fibres have been woven together to create a firm fabric. Some woven fabrics can have a little bit of stretch if they are mixed with a synthetic fibre, but usually woven fabrics are firm. Woven fabrics are very stable to sew with because the seams won't become wavy or stretch out while you're sewing, but the cut edges will fray over time and should be neatened (see techniques section).

The weight of a fabric refers to how thick the fabric is – for example denim and linen are heavy weight cottons, drill is middle weight cotton and poplin is light weight cotton. Knits too come in varying weights.

Fabrics are composed of natural fibres such as cotton, linen, or silk; or synthetic fibres such as polyester, nylon or acrylic; or a blend of natural and synthetic fibres. Natural fibres are great for hot summer days as they will allow your skin to breathe, but they do get very wrinkly after wearing them for a while. Knit fabrics are equally great but for different reasons – stretch fabrics are very comfortable to wear and they don't need ironing!

For each project throughout the book suggested fabric types and weights are listed for your reference. Think about how you want your finished project to look and feel: if you want a floaty and cool top choose a lightweight fabric, but if you want a sturdy beach bag, use a firm heavy weight fabric.

TOOLS AND TECHNIQUES

TECHNIQUES

The right side of the fabric: refers to the fabric that will be on the outside of your finished item of clothing. Usually, when you sew two layers of fabric together it's done with the right sides of the fabric facing, so that the seam and raw edges of the fabric are on the inside and can't be seen.

Backstitching: when sewing a seam, it's necessary to start by sewing a few stitches forwards, then backwards and then forwards again for the rest of the seam to secure the beginning of the seam, this technique is then repeated at the end of the seam. Backstitching saves you tying knots in your threads.

Pinning: pinning your fabrics together before sewing is really important to make sure the edges stay lined up when you are feeding the fabric through your sewing machine. Make sure you remove the pin before it goes under the sewing machine needle, otherwise it may break the needle. If you are sewing with striped fabric use lots of pins more closely spaced together to keep the stripes lined up.

Stitch types: Most sewing machines have a lot of different stitches. The majority of those stitches are decorative, but there are a few basic stitch types that are really useful for sewing clothes.

A *straight stitch* is the standard stitch and is best used on woven fabrics. A stitch length of about 2.5mm is usual for sewing seams, although you should check your machine's manual. A longer stitch length can be used to baste seams together temporarily, for example when you're just checking the fit, because a long stitch can be more easily removed.

A *zig zag stitch* is a stretch stitch that sews side to side and can be sewn in a variety of widths and lengths for different purposes. A longer stitch length with a narrow width can be used to sew the seams of knit fabrics, or a shorter stitch length with a wider width can be used to finish a raw seam edge if you don't have an overlocker, by sewing the zig zag very close to the edge of the fabric.

A *lightning stitch* is also a stretch stitch, and is a narrow and long zig zag stitch that some sewing machines have specifically for use on stretch fabrics so that the stitch will stretch with the fabric and the thread won't break. If your machine doesn't have this stitch, use a zig zag stitch instead if you're sewing a knit fabric.

A *twin stitch* uses a special double needle that can be sewn either in a straight stitch or a zig zag stitch. Twin stitching must be sewn on the right side of the fabric, because the underside of the stitching is a zig zag. Twin stitching is a great stitch for hems and around necklines on both stretch and woven fabrics.

An *overlock stitch* is made using an overlocker and can be used for finishing the raw edges of cut fabrics and for the actual seams. It cuts the fabric, while sewing a straight stitch and wrapping thread around the raw edge to stop the fabric fraying.

Pressing seams open or to one side: after sewing a seam, it is important to press a seam flat. Pressing just means ironing, except you press it onto the fabric, lift and press again instead of sliding the iron over your fabric. Seams are usually pressed open, or pressed to one side depending on the seam being sewn.

Neatening raw edges: the cut edges of woven fabric will fray due to the loose weave of the fabric, unless you neaten the raw edge. The easiest and quickest way is to overlock the edges of fabric, and some sewing machines have an overlocker type stitch that can be used if you don't have an overlocker. Otherwise, you can sew with a zig zag stitch close to the cut edge, or cut the edge with pinking shears.

TOOLS AND TECHNIQUES

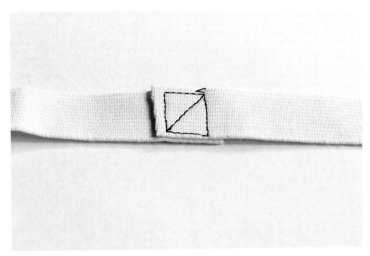

Joining ends of elastic: the flattest and most secure way of joining the ends of elastic is to overlap one end over the other by a few centimetres/ an inch, and then sewing through both layers in a square shape.

Turning a tube of fabric: because you sew a tube of fabric with the right sides of the fabric facing, you'll need to turn it the right way out. There are a few ways to do this:

If the tube is wide enough, you can use your fingers to slowly turn the fabric the right way out.

Another way is to attach a safety pin to one end of the tube, with the head of the safety pin inside the tube. Push the safety pin into the tube of fabric, bunching the tube up and then sliding the fabric over the safety pin as you go.

The quickest and easiest way however is to buy a loop turner. To use a loop turner, you slide the long point through the tube of fabric, and latch the hook at the end of the turner onto the fabric at the end of the tube. Pulling gently on the other end, slide the tube over the end that is hooked onto the tube turner, and keep pulling and sliding until the fabric comes out of the tube at the other end, the right way out.

About the patterns in this book

Choosing a size: pick the pattern size closest to your body measurements. If you are making a top, pick the pattern size according to your bust measurement, and if you're making a pair of pants use your hip size. If you are making a dress, it is likely you might need to blend two different sizes together to get a pattern that will match your measurements more closely.

Size	Bust	Waist	Hips
8	80 cm / 31½ in	66 cm / 26 in	90 cm / 35½ in
10	84 cm / 33 in	70 cm / 27½ in	94 cm / 37 in
12	88 cm / 34½ in	74 cm / 29¼ in	98 cm / 38½ in
14	92 cm / 36¼ in	78 cm / 30½ in	102 cm / 40¼ in

Making a pattern: The easiest way to make the pattern templates in this book full size is to go to a copy shop and have the relevant pattern enlarged to A0 size (except for the pencil skirt and shoulder bag pattern which should be enlarged to A1 size and the sun hat pattern which should be enlarged to A3 size). The patterns include seam and hem allowances.

The patterns show the cutting lines for all four sizes – the innermost dashed line is a size 8, the next solid line is a size 10, the next dashed line is a size 12 and the outermost solid line is a size 14. If your bust, waist and hip measurements are different sizes according to the chart above, you can blend the sizes you need to get a more accurate fit.

Template example:

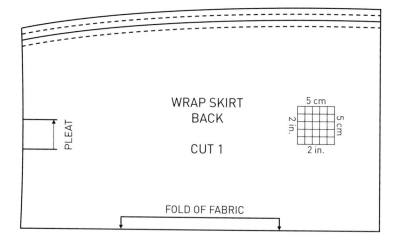

TOOLS AND TECHNIQUES

SEVERAL OF THE PATTERNS COMBINE TWO PROJECTS IN ONE, AS DESCRIBED BELOW:

- THE HALTER NECK DRESS AND MAXI DRESS;

- DRAPE NECK TOP AND DRESS;

- KAFTAN TOP AND MAXI DRESS;

- SIMPLE SHORTS AND PANTS;

- SINGLET TOP AND DRESS.

ALL PATTERNS CAN BE FOUND IN THE TEMPLATES SECTION AT THE BACK OF THE BOOK (PAGE 94–111).

Wrap Skirt

A wrap skirt is as simple to wear as it is to sew. This skirt has overlapping front panels to make sure that you don't accidentally show too much skin and the waistband ties mean you can tie the skirt as tight or loose as you like.

MATERIALS AND EQUIPMENT

• Lightweight woven fabrics such as cotton and cotton blend poplin, batiste, lawn, gingham etc.

• One press stud

CUTTING OUT

See templates section pages 94–95 for patterns

• Cut 2 pieces of the front skirt panel

• Cut 1 piece of the back skirt panel on a fold

• Cut two strips of fabric 65cm (25½ in) by 6cm (2½ in) for the ties

Sewing Instructions

STEP 1

Make the ties: Fold the strips of fabric in half lengthways with the right sides of the fabric facing. Sew along the long edge, 1cm (½ in) from the raw edge of the fabric to create a long tube. Turn the tube the right side out using the method described in the Tools and Techniques section.

STEP 2

Tuck in the raw edges of one end of the tube to the inside, press flat and sew across the edge to enclose the end.

STEP 3

Sew one tie to the side seam of one of the front skirt panels, 3cm (1¼ in) from the top edge, with the raw edge of the tie aligned with the raw edge of the side seam. This panel will become the inside front layer of the skirt.

STEP 4

Sew the side seams: Sew the front skirt panels to the back skirt panel at the side seams, with the right sides of the fabric facing and sewing 1cm (½ in) from the raw edge. Neaten the raw edges of the sewn seams and press the seams flat.

STEP 5

Make the pleats: Make the pleats at the waistband edge by bringing the marked lines together in the direction of the arrows marked on the pattern and sewing across the top through the folded fabric and the outer layer to secure the pleat. Press the pleats flat.

STEP 6

Sew around the outside edge: Neaten the raw edge of the top, the hem and the sides of the skirt. Fold the edges down 2cm (¾ in) towards the inside and press flat. On the right side, sew around the edge of the skirt 2cm (¾ in) from the folded edge, making sure you sew through both layers.

STEP 7

Attach the tie: Sew the remaining tie to the waistband of the outside front skirt panel.

STEP 8

Sew on the press-studs: Try on the skirt and tie it up securely. Mark the point where the top corner of the under layer of the front skirt panel finishes on the outer layer of the front skirt panel. Handsew a press stud to the inside of the skirt to join the two layers.

TIPS AND OPTIONS

INSTEAD OF MAKING TIES FOR THE SKIRT FROM THE FABRIC, YOU COULD USE NARROW RIBBON INSTEAD.

Pencil Skirt

A pencil skirt is one of those fashion basics that have a place in every wardrobe. Worn with flat sandals and a cute top it's the perfect smart casual outfit, but put on some heels and a shirt and you could wear your pencil skirt to the office in style. Choose a thicker knit fabric that still has a good amount of stretch so that you get a close fit but still have enough stretch to walk comfortably.

MATERIALS AND EQUIPMENT

• Stretch fabrics such as jersey knit or double knit

• Elastic 25mm (1 in) wide

CUTTING OUT

See templates section page 96 for pattern

Fold your fabric in half lengthways. Cut out the pattern piece twice, with the straight edge along the fold of the fabric.

Sewing Instructions

STEP 1

Sew the side seams: Place the two pieces of fabric together with the right sides of the fabric facing each other.

STEP 2

Pin and sew the side seams 1cm (½ in) from the cut edges, sewing from the top to the bottom. Press the seam flat open.

STEP 3

Sew the waistband: Cut a piece of elastic that is long enough to fit snugly around your waist plus 2cm (¾ in). Sew the ends of the elastic together by overlapping the ends and sewing a small square, as described in the Tools and Techniques chapter.

STEP 4

Mark the elastic into 4 equal quarters using pins. Place each pin at the side seam, centre front and centre back of the top of the skirt and pin the elastic to the inside of the skirt.

STEP 5

Sew the elastic to the top of the fabric using a stretch stitch, stretch the elastic slightly between the points as you sew. Turn the elastic down to the inside of the fabric, on the right side of the fabric sew the entire way around the waistband using a straight stitch, close to the bottom edge of the elastic.

STEP 6

Sew the hem: Fold up 2cm (¾ in) of the fabric to the inside at the bottom edge of the skirt and press flat. On the right side of the fabric, sew the entire way around the bottom of the skirt 2cm (¾ in) from the folded edge using a stretch stitch or a twin needle stitch.

TIPS AND OPTIONS

- TRY ON THE SKIRT TO CHECK THE FIT BEFORE SEWING THE WAISTBAND – SOME FABRICS ARE STRETCHIER THAN OTHERS AND SOME PEOPLE PREFER A TIGHTER FIT, SO YOU MAY WANT TO SEW FURTHER FROM THE CUT EDGE TO MAKE YOUR SKIRT TIGHTER. IF YOUR SKIRT HAS TURNED OUT TOO TIGHT, UNPICK THE SEAM AND SEW CLOSER TO THE CUT EDGE TO GIVE MORE ROOM.

- IF YOU FIND SOME COLOURFUL OR DECORATIVE ELASTIC THAT WOULD LOOK GOOD WITH YOUR FABRIC, YOU COULD SEW AN EXPOSED ELASTIC WAISTBAND. FOLLOW THE INSTRUCTIONS FOR THE STRAPLESS TOP TO DO THIS.

- YOU DON'T HAVE TO SEW THE HEM IF YOU WANT A MORE CASUAL LOOK. THE KNIT FABRIC WON'T FRAY, BUT IT MAY ROLL A LITTLE AFTER A FEW WEARS.

Gathered Skirt

This gathered skirt is a variation on the traditional dirndl skirt, but this version has a comfortable elastic waistband. Lighter fabrics will gather and hang close to the body, but if you choose a stiffer or thicker fabric your skirt will be fuller and have a lovely vintage vibe.

MATERIALS AND EQUIPMENT

- Lightweight or mid-weight woven fabrics such as cotton and cotton blend poplin, batiste, lawn, gingham, chambray, sateen etc.

- Elastic 25mm (1 in) or wider, cut to the width of your waist measurement

- Safety pin

CUTTING OUT

Cut two rectangles of fabric that have a width of your hip measurement plus 2cm (¾ in) seam allowance and a length of the distance from your waist to the point where you want your skirt to finish, plus 6cm (2⅜ in) for the waistband and hem.

Sewing Instructions

STEP 1

Sew the side seams: Sew the two rectangles of fabric together with the right sides of the fabric facing each other, along the shorter edge of the rectangles. Neaten the raw edges of the sewn seam, and press the seam flat.

STEP 2

Sew the waistband: Fold the top edge down towards the inside by 0.5cm (¼ in) and press flat. Then fold the edge down another 3cm (1¼ in) (fold it down more if you are using wider elastic) towards the inside and press flat. This will create a waistband casing for the elastic and enclose the raw edge.

STEP 3

On the right side, sew around the waistband 3cm (1¼ in) down from the top edge using a straight stitch, making sure you are sewing through the folded down fabric on the inside as well as the outside layer. Stop sewing about 4cm (1½ in) from where you started sewing to leave a small gap.

STEP 4

Pin the safety pin to one end of the elastic, and slide it into the waistband casing through the small gap. Keep sliding the elastic through the waistband casing by pushing the safety pin through the tube, the entire way around and out the small gap again. Make sure you keep the other end of the elastic out of the casing – it helps to pin the free end to the skirt to stop it being pulled in.

STEP 5

Pull the two ends of the elastic out of the waistband casing far enough to give yourself room to work with, and sew the two ends of the elastic together by overlapping the ends using the technique explained in the Tools and Techniques chapter. Push the elastic back into the waistband casing and then on the right side sew the small gap closed.

STEP 6

Sew the hem: Neaten the raw edge of the bottom of the skirt, fold the fabric towards the inside by 3cm (1¼ in) and press flat. On the right side, sew around the hem close to the edge of the folded up fabric.

TIPS AND OPTIONS

- THE WIDTH OF THE FABRIC DETERMINES HOW FULL YOUR SKIRT IS — IF YOU WANT THE SKIRT MORE GATHERED CUT THE RECTANGLES WIDER, AND IF YOU WANT LESS GATHERS, CUT THE RECTANGLE LESS WIDE BUT MAKE SURE THAT THE TOTAL WIDTH OF THE SKIRT, WHEN THE FRONT AND BACK ARE SEWN TOGETHER, ARE AT LEAST 20CM (8 IN) WIDER THAN YOUR HIP MEASUREMENT FOR WEARING EASE AND TO HAVE SOME GATHERS.

- YOU COULD SEW SOME RECTANGLE OR SQUARE PATCH POCKETS ON THE SKIRT AT THE FRONT OR THE BACK, OR SEW SOME POCKETS IN THE SIDE SEAMS USING THE PATTERN PIECE AND INSTRUCTIONS FROM THE PATTERN FOR THE SHORTS PROJECT (SEE PAGE XX). SEW THE POCKET PIECES TO THE SIDES OF THE SKIRT PANELS BEFORE STEP 1.

- SEW SOME RIBBON OR TRIM AROUND THE SKIRT NEAR THE HEM, OR SEW A BAND OF FABRIC IN A CONTRASTING COLOUR TO THE BOTTOM HEM.

GATHERED SKIRT

Strapless Maxi Dress

A strapless maxi dress is a glamourous look for the poolside and for shopping trips, whilst being supremely comfortable. By sewing this dress for yourself you can make it exactly as long as you need it, no more too long maxi dresses that need hitching up when you walk!

MATERIALS AND EQUIPMENT

- Stretchy knit fabric such as jersey, lycra blends or rayon polyester knits

- 25mm (1 in) elastic

CUTTING OUT

Cut a rectangle of fabric that is one and a half times your hip width, and the length measured from your armpit to your ankle, plus 5cm (2 in).

Sewing Instructions

STEP 1

Sew the side seam: Fold the fabric in half lengthways, with the right sides of the fabric facing. Sew down the side seam, 1cm (½ in) from the raw edge. Press the seam flat.

STEP 2

Sew the elastic: Cut a length of elastic that will fit snugly around your chest under your armpits, plus 2cm (¾ in). Sew the ends of the elastic together as described in the Tools and Techniques section. Mark the elastic at 4 equal quarter points.

STEP 3

Sew the top of the dress: Mark the top of the dress into 4 equal points, with the side seam being one. Pin the elastic to the inside of the top of the dress, matching the 4 marked points of the elastic to the 4 marked points of the dress.

STEP 4

Using a stretch stitch, sew the elastic to the dress, stretching the elastic slightly between the points marked.

STEP 5

Fold the elastic down towards the inside of the dress, on the right side of the fabric stitch the entire way around the top of the dress 2cm (¾ in) from the top, making sure you are sewing through the top layer and the elastic. Use a stretch stitch or a twin stitch needle.

STEP 6

Sew the hem: fold the fabric up 2.5cm (1 in) towards the inside of the dress at the bottom and press flat. Sew around the hem using a stretch stitch or with a twin stitch needle.

TIPS AND OPTIONS

- MAKE A BELT FOR YOUR MAXI DRESS USING A NARROW STRIP OF LEFT-OVER FABRIC, OR SEW A NARROW WIDTH ELASTIC AROUND THE INSIDE OF THE DRESS AT THE WAISTLINE TO GIVE THE DRESS MORE SHAPE.

- YOU DON'T NEED TO SEW A HEM ON YOUR DRESS IF YOU DON'T WANT TO - KNIT FABRIC WON'T FRAY, BUT IT MAY START TO ROLL A LITTLE AFTER A FEW WEARS.

- IF YOU WOULD LIKE A CLOSER FITTING MAXI DRESS OR YOU ARE USING REALLY STRETCHY FABRIC, CUT THE FABRIC TO YOUR HIP WIDTH PLUS 10CM (4 IN) TO ALLOW FOR SEAM ALLOWANCE AND WEARING EASE. FINISH SEWING THE SIDE SEAM AT YOUR KNEE LEVEL AND LEAVE OPEN FOR WALKING EASE.

Drawstring Pants

Drawstring pants are wide legged and loose fitting, they are also comfortable to wear as pyjama pants but when made in dress fabrics such as linen they are a classic and stylish look. If you do want some pyjama pants, this pattern will work equally well if you use a cute fabric, or even flannelette for some warm winter pyjamas.

MATERIALS AND EQUIPMENT

• Lightweight woven fabrics such as cotton and cotton blend poplin, linen, batiste, lawn, gingham etc.

• ribbon or cord for the drawstring

• safety pin

CUTTING OUT

See templates section pages 100–101 for pattern

Fold your fabric in half so that there are two layers of fabric. Cut out two pieces of the front and back legs each.

Sewing Instructions

STEP 1

Sew the leg seams: Lay one front leg piece over a back leg piece, with the right sides of the fabric facing each other. Pin and sew the outside leg seam and the inside leg seam. Do the same with the other pieces.

STEP 2

Neaten the edges of the sewn leg seams, and iron the seams flat open.

STEP 3

Turn one leg the right way out, so that the seams are on the inside. Leave the other leg inside out, so that the seams are on the outside.

STEP 4

Sew the legs together: Slide the leg piece that has been turned the right way out inside the other leg piece so that the right sides of the fabric are facing each other. Match up the top of the front leg, the side seam and the top of the back leg – this should form a "u" shape. Pin and sew from the top of the front legs to the top of the back legs.

STEP 5

Pull the inside leg out of the other one and turn the pants the right way out – they should now look like proper pants with two legs! Iron the centre front seam flat.

STEP 6

Sew the drawstring slits: At the centre front, 4.5cm (1¾ in) down from the top edge, on either side of the centre front seam sew a buttonhole (check your sewing machine user manual to see how to do this) or sew a small rectangle using a straight stitch. Make small cuts inside the buttonhole or rectangle you've sewn to create small openings for your drawstring to come through.

STEP 7

Sew the waistband: Turn down the top edge of the pants 1cm (½ in) and iron flat – this will keep the raw edge hidden when the waistband is folded down again and sewn. Then fold down the waistband another 2.5cm (1 in) from the top to the inside of the pants and iron flat, to form a casing for the drawstring. On the right side of the fabric, sew entirely around the top of the pants 2.5cm (1 in) down from the top, making sure you catch the folded edge on the inside.

STEP 8

Insert the drawstring: Stick a safety pin in one end of the cord and slide through one of the openings in the front of the pants. Push the safety pin through the casing and out of the other opening. Pull the cord through so that there is an equal amount of cord hanging out of both openings.

STEP 9

Sew the hems: Try on the pants and work out how long you need them. Fold up the bottom of the legs to the inside of the pants to the length you need and sew around the outside.

TIPS AND OPTIONS

- IF YOU LIKE YOUR CLOTHES WITH POCKETS, YOU COULD SEW SOME RECTANGLE OR SQUARE PATCH POCKETS ON THE PANTS AT THE BACK, OR SEW SOME POCKETS IN THE SIDE SEAMS USING THE PATTERN PIECE AND INSTRUCTIONS FROM THE PATTERN FOR THE SHORTS PROJECT (SEE PAGE 97). SEW THE POCKET PIECES TO THE SIDES OF EACH PANTS LEG BEFORE STEP 1.

Singlet Dress and Top

A simple singlet dress is the easiest "put on and go" outfit, just add shoes and you're ready to head out the door in no time. A singlet top is also a great basic to pair with the skirts and pants projects in this book, or wear with faded jean shorts for a classic summer beach look.

MATERIALS AND EQUIPMENT

Stretch knit fabrics such as jersey knit, interlock or double knit

CUTTING OUT

See templates section page 98–99 for pattern

Note that the pattern template is the same for both the singlet top and dress – cut the singlet top at the marked line, and for the dress cut the pattern out to its full length.

Fold your fabric in half, with the stretch of the fabric going across from the folded edge to the cut edges.

Place the straight edge of the pattern pieces along the folded edge, cut out one each of the front and back pattern pieces.
Cut out 3 rectangles from the same fabric or a different coloured stretch fabric, 1 piece 4cm (1½ in) wide by 65cm (26 in) long for the neck band, and 2 pieces 4cm (1½ in) cm wide by 35cm (14 in) long for the sleeve bands.

Sewing instructions

Instructions are the same for the top and dress, the only difference is in the length of fabric for each project.

STEP 1

Sew the side and shoulder seams: Lay the front piece on the back piece, with the right sides of the fabric facing each other. Pin and sew the shoulder seams and side seams, using a stretch stitch and sewing 1cm (½ in) from the raw edge. On the inside, press these seams flat open.

STEP 2

Sew the neck and arm bands: Sew the short ends of the rectangle bands together with the right sides of the fabric facing each other, and press this seam flat open. Fold the band in half lengthwise with the right side of the fabric on the outside and iron the folded edge flat.

STEP 3

Sew the neck band to the top: Mark the neckband into two equal points. Pin the neck band to the neckline on the right side of the fabric, matching the marked points to the shoulder seams. Gently stretch the neck band to match the length of the neck edge, and pin the neck band evenly stretched to the neckline, with the cut edges matching. Sew around the neckline 1cm (½ in) from the cut edge. Flip the neck band up and the seam allowance down, press this flat.

STEP 4

To make sure the neck band stays up and the seam allowance doesn't flip out, on the right side of the fabric sew around the neckline just underneath the neckband seam, through both the outside fabric layer and the seam allowance, using a twin stitch needle or a stretch stitch.

STEP 5

Sew the sleeve band to the top: Sew on the band in the same way as the neck band.

STEP 6

Sew the hem: Fold the bottom edge of the t-shirt up 2cm (¾ in) on the inside and iron the folded edge flat. On the right side of the fabric, sew all around the hem 2cm (¾ in) from the bottom edge of the fabric using either a twin stitch or a stretch stitch, making sure you catch the seam allowance on the inside.

TIPS AND OPTIONS

NECKBANDS WILL NEED TO BE ABOUT 5CM (2 IN) SHORTER THAN THE OPENING, BUT IF YOUR FABRIC IS VERY STRETCHY YOU MAY NEED TO CUT THE NECK AND SLEEVE BANDS SHORTER. MAKE SURE YOU CAN STILL GET THE NECKBAND OVER YOUR HEAD THOUGH!

Strapless Shirred Dress

Shirred fabric is simply fabric that has been gathered by multiple lines of elastic thread, it looks much more complicated than it actually is. Shirring is a cute way to add shape to a dress bodice while still keeping the skirt full and floaty. You can make this pattern as long as you like, keep it short for a top or make it long for a maxi dress.

MATERIALS AND EQUIPMENT

• Lightweight woven fabric such as cotton and cotton blend poplin, batiste, lawn, gingham, sateen etc.

• Elastic Thread

• 25mm (1 in) elastic

CUTTING OUT

Cut a rectangle of fabric that is twice as wide as your hip measurement, and as long as you want when measured from under your armpit plus 5cm (2 in). If your fabric isn't wide enough, cut two rectangles (one for the front and one for the back).

Sewing Instructions

STEP 1

Sew the side seam: Fold the fabric in half with right sides together and sew down the side seam. Neaten the raw edges of this seam and press the seam flat.

STEP 2

Sew the top edge: Neaten the raw edge of the fabric at the top. Fold this edge 3cm (1¼ in) down to the inside of the fabric and press flat. Sew around the top of the dress 3cm (1¼ in) from the top edge of the fabric, catching the folded down fabric on the inside, stopping 4cm (1½ in) from the point where you started stitching. This will create a casing to insert the elastic into later.

STEP 3

Sew the shirring lines: Wind the elastic thread onto the bobbin by hand, pulling it slightly but not winding it too tight. Put your bobbin in your machine in the normal way. Keep your normal sewing thread in the machine needle.

STEP 4

On the right side of the fabric, sew 15 straight lines the whole way around the fabric 1cm (½ in) apart, starting below the casing for the elastic. You can mark lines on the fabric using tailors chalk to be accurate, or you can just use the edge of the presser foot to keep the lines evenly spaced – it's not important to be exact because when the fabric is gathered up it won't be noticeable.

STEP 5

Once you have sewn the entire way around the fabric, tie the tail end of the elastic thread with the beginning of the thread with a few tight knots to secure it. Do this for each line of sewing.

STEP 6

Insert elastic to the top edge: Cut a length of elastic to fit snugly around your chest under your armpits. Slide this elastic through the fabric casing at the top of the fabric, sew the ends together and sew the gap closed.

STEP 7

Sew the hem: Neaten the raw edge of the bottom of the fabric, and turn this up 2cm (¾ in) to the inside of the fabric. Press this flat. On the right side of the fabric using normal sewing thread in both the needle and the bobbin, sew all the way around the hem of the fabric using a straight stitch.

STRAPLESS SHIRRED DRESS

TIPS AND OPTIONS

- MAKE THE LENGTH OF THE SHIRRED SECTION AS LONG AS YOU WANT – ALL THE WAY TO YOUR WAISTLINE FOR A MORE FITTED SILHOUETTE, OR JUST A SHORT AMOUNT OVER YOUR BUST LINE TO CREATE A MORE FLOWING DRESS.

- THE ELASTIC AT THE TOP IS JUST FOR EXTRA SECURITY, BUT YOU CAN LEAVE IT OFF IF YOU WANT TO – THE LINES OF SHIRRING SHOULD HOLD THE DRESS UP WELL ENOUGH WITHOUT IT.

- EVERY SEWING MACHINE IS DIFFERENT AND FOR SOME REASON SOME SEWING MACHINES SHIRR FABRIC BETTER THAN OTHERS.

- WHEN SEWING THE SHIRRING LINES, USE THE LONGEST STRAIGHT STITCH WITH NORMAL TENSION.

- LIGHTWEIGHT FABRICS WORK BEST FOR SHIRRING, THE THICKER THE FABRIC THE LESS IT WILL GATHER.

- THE MORE ROWS OF SHIRRING YOU SEW THE MORE GATHERED IT WILL BE, SO DON'T WORRY IF IT DOESN'T LOOK GATHERED ENOUGH TO START WHEN YOU'VE ONLY DONE A FEW ROWS.

- WHEN YOU'VE FINISHED SEWING THE SHIRRING LINES, HOLD A STEAM IRON CLOSE TO THE FABRIC BUT MAKE SURE IT IS NOT TOUCHING AND STEAM THE LINES TO HELP IT SHRINK FURTHER. YOU CAN ALSO PUT IT IN A WARM DRYER AFTER WASHING TO HELP SHRINK THE FABRIC A LITTLE.

STRAPLESS SHIRRED DRESS

Simple Shorts

These simple shorts are really useful for those times when you're exercising or doing something adventurous and a floaty skirt or dress just won't do. You could even make these into a cute pair of pyjama shorts.

MATERIAL AND EQUIPMENT

- Lightweight woven fabrics such as cotton and cotton blend poplin, batiste, lawn, gingham, chambray, sateen etc, or knit fabrics such as cotton jersey or interlock

- 25mm (1in) wide elastic

CUTTING OUT

See templates section page 102–103 for pattern

Note that this pattern is the same as the pattern for the lightweight pants – make sure you cut along the marked line on the leg pattern pieces for the shorts.

Cut out two each of the front and back patterns

Cut out four pocket pieces. Create a pattern for the pocket piece by tracing the pocket from the front leg pattern piece.

Sewing Instructions

STEP 1

Sewing the pockets: Pin one pocket piece on each of the front and back pieces, with right sides of the fabric facing and the straight edge of the pocket lined up with the side of the front and back pieces in the position marked on the pattern. Using a straight stitch for a woven fabric or a stretch stitch for a knit fabric, sew the straight edges of the pocket pieces to the front and back pieces.

STEP 2

Sew the outside side seams: Lay one front piece on top of one back piece with the right sides of the fabric facing, lining up the side seams and the pocket pieces. Pin the front to the back along the side seam and around the pocket.

STEP 3

Using a straight stitch for a woven fabric or a stretch stitch for a knit fabric, sew the side seams 1cm (½ in) from the edges of the fabric, stopping at the pocket piece. With the sewing machine needle down in the fabric, lift the presser foot and turn the fabric around and sew around the curved edge of the pocket piece. When you reach the side seam, with the sewing machine needle down in the fabric, lift the presser foot and turn the fabric around again and sew

straight down the rest of the side seam (see technique on templates page 97).

STEP 4

Neaten the raw edge of the sewn seam if you are using a woven fabric, and press the seam open.

STEP 5

Sew the inner leg seams: With the right sides of the fabric facing, pin the side seam at the inner leg. Using a straight stitch for a woven fabric or a stretch stitch for a knit fabric, sew down the seam 1cm (½ in) from the edge. Neaten the raw edge of the sewn seam if you are using a woven fabric, and press the seam open.

STEP 6

Sew the centre front and centre back seam: Turn one of the shorts legs the right side out, and slide this one inside the other shorts leg so that the right sides of the fabric are facing. Pin the two layers together, matching the inner leg seams and the top of the front and back. Using a straight stitch for a woven fabric or a stretch stitch for a knit fabric, sew this 'u shaped' seam. Neaten the raw edge of the sewn seam if you are using a woven fabric, and press the seam open.

STEP 7

Sew the waistband: If using using a woven fabric, first neaten the top edge of the shorts.

STEP 8

Cut a length of elastic so that it fits snugly around your waist plus 2cm (¾ in). Sew the ends of the elastic together by overlapping the ends as described in the Tools and Techniques section. Mark the elastic into 4 equal quarters using pins or a small pen mark.

STEP 9

On the inside of the shorts, pin the elastic to the fabric matching the four points marked on the elastic to the side seams and the centre front and centre back seams.

STEP 10

Starting at one marked point with the machine needle down in the fabric, hold on to the fabric and elastic behind the machine needle with one hand and the next marked point in your other hand. Gently stretch the elastic away from the machine needle until it is the same length as the fabric between the two quarter points. Using a stretch stitch, sew the elastic to the top of the shorts close to the top edge. When you reach the marked point, leave the machine needle down in the fabric and continue gently stretching the fabric so that you can sew the entire way around the top of the waistband.

STEP 11

Fold the elastic down on the inside of the shorts so that the elastic is no longer visible.

On the right side of the fabric, sew around the waistband close to the bottom edge of the folded down elastic using a stretch stitch.

STEP 12

Sew the hems: If you are using a woven fabric, first neaten the raw edges of the hems. Fold up the hem of each leg by 3cm (1¼ in) and press the folded edge flat. On the right side of the fabric, sew the hem 3cm (1¼ in) from the bottom using a straight stitch for a woven fabric or a stretch stitch for a knit fabric.

TIPS AND OPTIONS

- TO MAKE THIS QUICKER AND AN EVEN EASIER PROJECT YOU CAN LEAVE THE POCKETS OFF AND SIMPLY SEW THE SIDE SEAMS STRAIGHT DOWN FROM THE TOP TO THE BOTTOM. YOU COULD SEW ON SQUARE PATCH POCKETS ON EACH SIDE OF THE BACK OF THE SHORTS INSTEAD IF YOU STILL NEED SOME POCKETS.

Lightweight Pants

These slouchy pants are slightly tapered in the leg, and are a comfortable and casual alternative to traditional pants. You could dress them up with heels and a fitted top for a glam look, or make them in a wild print to wear with sandals for a more casual outfit.

MATERIAL AND EQUIPMENT

- Stretch knit fabric such as jersey

- 25mm (1 in) wide elastic

CUTTING OUT

See templates section page 102–103 for pattern

Note that this pattern is the same as the pattern for the simple shorts – this project uses the full-length leg pattern pieces.

Cut out two each of the front and back pattern pieces.

Cut out four pocket pieces. Create a pattern for the pocket piece by tracing the pocket from the front leg pattern piece.

Sewing Instructions

STEP 1

Sewing the pockets: Pin one pocket piece on each of the front and back pieces, with right sides of the fabric facing and the straight edge of the pocket lined up with the side of the front and back pieces in the position marked on the pattern. Using a straight stitch for a woven fabric or a stretch stitch for a knit fabric, sew the straight edges of the pocket pieces to the front and back.

STEP 2

Sew the outside side seams: Lay one front piece on top of one back piece, right sides of fabric facing, lining up the side seams and the pocket pieces. Pin the front to the back along the side seam and around the pocket.

STEP 3

Using a straight stitch for a woven fabric or a stretch stitch for a knit fabric, sew the side seams 1cm (½ in) from the edges of the fabric, stopping at the pocket piece. With the sewing machine needle down in the fabric, lift the presser foot and turn the fabric around and sew around the curved edge of the pocket piece. When you reach the side seam, with the sewing machine needle down in the fabric, lift the presser foot and turn the fabric around again and sew straight down the rest of the side seam.

STEP 4

Neaten raw edge of sewn seam if using a woven fabric, and press the seam open.

STEP 5

Sew the inner leg seams: With the right sides of the fabric facing, pin the side seam at the inner leg. Using a straight stitch for a woven fabric or a stretch stitch for a knit fabric, sew down the seam 1cm (½ in) from the edge. Neaten the raw edge of the sewn seam if you are using a woven fabric, and press the seam open.

STEP 6

Sew the centre front and centre back seam: Turn one of the legs the right side out, and slide this one inside the other leg so that the right sides of the fabric are facing. Pin the two layers together, matching the inner leg seams and the top of the front and back. Using a straight stitch for a woven fabric or a stretch stitch for a knit fabric, sew this 'u shaped' seam. Neaten the raw edge of the sewn seam if you are using a woven fabric, and press the seam open.

STEP 7

Sew the waistband: If using a woven fabric, first neaten the top edge of the shorts. Cut a length of elastic so that it fits snugly around your waist plus 2cm (¾ in). Sew the ends of the elastic together by overlapping the ends as described in the Tools and Techniques section. Mark the elastic into 4 equal quarter points using pins or a small pen mark.

STEP 9

On the inside of the pants, pin the elastic to the fabric matching the four points marked on the elastic to the side seams and the centre front and centre back seams.

STEP 10

Starting at one marked point with the machine needle down in the fabric, hold on to the fabric and elastic behind the machine needle with one hand and the next marked point in your other hand. Gently stretch the elastic away from the machine needle until it is the same length as the fabric between the two quarter points. Using a stretch stitch, sew the elastic to the top of the pants close to the top edge. When you reach the marked point, leave the machine needle down in the fabric and continue gently stretching the fabric so that you can sew the entire way around the top of the waistband.

STEP 11

Fold the elastic down on the inside of the pants so it is no longer visible. On the right side of the fabric, sew around the waistband close to the bottom edge of the folded down elastic using a stretch stitch.

STEP 12

Sew the hems: If you are using a woven fabric, first neaten the raw edges of the hems. Fold up the hem of each leg by 3cm (1 ¼ in) and press the folded edge flat. On the right side of the fabric, sew the hem 3cm (1 ¼ in) from the bottom using a straight stitch for a woven fabric or a stretch stitch for a knit fabric.

STEP 13

Sew the hem cuffs: Cut a length of elastic slightly bigger than your ankle plus 2cm (1 in). Sew the elastic into a loop by overlapping the ends by 2cm (1 in) as described in the Tools and Techniques section. Mark the elastic into 2 equal points.

STEP 14

Follow the waistband sewing instructions above to sew the elastic cuff of the bottom of each pant leg, matching the two marked points to the side seams.

TIPS AND OPTIONS

TO MAKE THIS A QUICK AND EASY PROJECT, LEAVE THE POCKETS OFF AND SEW THE SIDE SEAMS STRAIGHT DOWN FROM THE TOP TO BOTTOM. YOU COULD SEW ON SQUARE PATCH POCKETS ON EACH SIDE OF THE BACK OF THE SHORTS IF YOU STILL NEED SOME POCKETS.

Strapless Top

This simple tube style top is designed with a line of gathering down the centre front to flatter and accentuate your shape. This is a great basic top to wear with the skirt and pants projects in this book, and is perfect to show off tanned shoulders.

MATERIAL AND EQUIPMENT

- Stretchy knit fabrics such as jersey, lycra, interlock or slinky knits

- 25mm (1 in) wide elastic

- 5mm (¼ in) wide elastic

CUTTING OUT

Cut a rectangle of fabric as wide as your bust measurement plus 2cm (¾ in), and as long as the distance measured from under your armpits to where you want your top to finish, plus 3cm (1¼ in) for a hem.

Sewing Instructions

STEP 1

Sew the side seam: Fold the fabric in half with the right sides facing each other. Sew the side seam using a stretch stitch, 2cm (¾ in) from the raw edge. Press the seam flat open.

STEP 2

Sew the elastic top: Cut a length of elastic to fit snugly around your chest just below your armpits, plus 2cm (¾ in). Sew the elastic into a tube by matching up the raw ends and sewing 1cm (½ in) from the ends. Press the elastic flat open using an iron on a low setting so that the elastic doesn't melt.

STEP 3

Mark the elastic into 4 equal quarter points and also mark the top into 4 equal quarter points.

STEP 4

Pin the elastic to the outside of the fabric, matching the four marked points. On the inside of the elastic, bring the fabric halfway up the width of the elastic, and on the right side of the elastic sew completely around the top using a straight stitch close to the bottom of the elastic. Stretch the elastic slightly between the points when sewing.

STEP 5

Sew the centre front elastic: With the side seam at one side, mark a line down the centre front of the top on the inside starting approximately 5cm (2 in) from underneath the elastic. On the inside, sew a short length of elastic to the fabric along this line, using a stretch stitch for about 5cm (2 in), stretching the elastic as much as possible whilst sewing. Backstitch a few times at the bottom to secure the elastic, and cut any excess elastic off.

STEP 6

Sew the hem: Turn up 3cm (1¼ in) of the bottom of the fabric to the inside this will create a hem. Press this flat, and sew around the bottom using a stretch stitch or a twin stitch needle.

TIPS AND OPTIONS

- IF YOU CAN'T FIND PATTERNED ELASTIC, SEW ELASTIC TO THE INSIDE OF THE FABRIC AND FOLD DOWN. (METHOD EXPLAINED IN STRAPLESS MAXI INSTRUCTIONS (SEE PAGE 29).

- IF YOUR WAIST MEASUREMENT IS LARGER THAN YOUR BUST, CUT FABRIC TO YOUR WAIST MEASUREMENT PLUS THE 2CM (¾ IN) FOR SEAM ALLOWANCE, SO THE TOP ISN'T TOO TIGHT AROUND YOUR WAIST. THE ELASTIC AT THE TOP WILL STILL HOLD THE TOP UP.

- YOU COULD SEW THE NARROW ELASTIC THE ENTIRE WAY DOWN THE CENTRE FROM THE TOP TO THE BOTTOM TO CREATE A RUCHED TOP — JUST ADD SOME EXTRA LENGTH AS THE ELASTIC WILL GATHER THE FABRIC UP SLIGHTLY.

- THE EASIEST WAY TO SEW THE LENGTH OF ELASTIC AT THE CENTRE FRONT IS TO HAVE AN EXTRA BIT OF ELASTIC AT THE TOP BEFORE SEWING SO YOU HAVE A SMALL LENGTH TO HOLD ON TO WHILE STRETCHING THE ELASTIC OUT AT THE OTHER END WITH YOUR OTHER HAND. WHEN YOU'VE FINISHED SEWING THE LINE SIMPLY CUT THE EXCESS OFF THE TOP AND THE BOTTOM.

Drape Neck Top and Dress

A drape neck top or dress is a sophisticated variation to a simple style. The top and dress are both slim fitting and have a flattering drape of fabric around the front neckline to add interest. This project has two variations, a short version to be worn as a top and a longer, dress length version.

MATERIALS

Stretch knit fabrics such as jersey, interlock or slinky knits.

CUTTING OUT

See templates section pages 104–105 for patterns

Note that the pattern template is the same for both the top and dress – cut at the marked lines for the top, and use the full-length pattern for the dress.

Fold your fabric in half with the stretch of the fabric going across the width of the fabric.

Cut one front and one back piece, with the straight edge of the pattern pieces against the fold as marked on the pattern.

Sewing Instructions

STEP 1

Sew the side and shoulder seams: Lay the front piece on the back piece, with the right sides of the fabric facing. Using a stretch stitch, sew the front to the back at the shoulder and side seams, stopping at the marked lines on the patterns. Press the seams flat open.

STEP 2

Finish the drape edge: Fold the raw edge of the neckline to the inside by 1cm (½ in), press flat. On the right side of the fabric sew around the neckline 1cm (½ in) from edge, using twin needle stitch or stretch stitch.

STEP 3

Finish the sleeve edges: Fold the raw edge of the sleeves to the inside by 1cm (½ in) and press flat. On the right side of the fabric sew around the sleeve edge 1cm (½ in) from the edge, using a twin needle stitch or a stretch stitch.

STEP 4

Fold the raw edge of the bottom hemline to the inside by 3cm (1¼ in) and press flat. On the right side of the fabric sew around the neckline 3cm (1¼ in) from the bottom edge using a twin needle stitch or a stretch stitch, making sure you catch the hem allowance on the inside.

TIPS AND OPTIONS

- KNIT FABRIC WILL NOT FRAY, SO IF YOU LIKE A CASUAL LOOK YOU DON'T NEED TO FINISH THE NECK OR SLEEVE EDGES OR SEW A HEM.

Halter Neck Dress

This simple dress is designed to show off lovely shoulders and arms. Make it in luxurious fabrics for an elegant evening dress, or in a simple cotton fabric for an easy daytime dress. This project has two variations, a short version and a maxi version with waistline detail.

MATERIALS AND EQUIPMENT

- Lightweight woven materials such as cotton and blends like poplin, batiste, lawn, gingham, or luxurious fabrics such as chiffon, georgette or beaded fabrics

- Narrow elastic

- Safety pin

CUTTING OUT

See templates section page 106 for patterns

Note that the pattern template is the same for both the short and long versions of this dress – cut the dress pattern at the marked lines for the shorter version, and for the longer version cut the length to your ankles.

Fold your fabric in half and cut out 2 pieces from the pattern piece, with the straight edge of the pattern along the folded edge of the fabric, as marked on the pattern.

Cut two strips of fabric 4cm (1½ in) by 75cm (29½ in) for the neck ties.

Sewing Instructions
For the short version:

STEP 1

Sew the side seams: Pin the two pieces of fabric together at the side seams with the right sides of the fabric facing. Sew the side seams, 1cm (½ in) from the edge. Neaten the raw edges and press the seam flat open.

STEP 2

Sew the armhole seams: Neaten the raw edges of the armhole seams, fold the fabric 1cm (½ in) to the inside and press flat. Sew 1cm (½ in) from the edge of the armhole seam, making sure you catch the seam allowance on the inside.

STEP 3

Sew the top edge: Neaten the raw edge of the top of the front and back panels of the dress. Fold the fabric 2.5cm (1 in) to the inside and press flat. Sew 2.5cm (1 in) from the edge of the top, making sure you catch the seam allowance on the inside. This will create a casing for the neck ties.

STEP 4

Sew the neck ties: Fold the two strips of fabric in half lengthways and sew 1cm (½ in) from the edge to create a long tube. Turn the tubes of fabric the right side out, following the method described in the Tools and Techniques section. With a safety pin at the end of the tie, slide the safety pin through the casing at the top of the dress until the tie is the entire way through. Do the same for the front and back casing.

STEP 5

Sew the hem: Neaten the raw edge of the bottom of the dress and fold the fabric 2.5cm (1 in) to the inside and press flat. Sew 2.5cm (1 in) from the edge of the top, making sure you catch the seam allowance on the inside.

HALTER NECK DRESS

For the maxi version:

Sew the maxi version as described for the short version, with the following changes:

STEP 1

Sew the side seams: Stop sewing the side seams about 45cm (17½ in) from the bottom to create open splits for walking ease. Press the seam flat open, and on the right side of the fabric sew 1cm (½ in) from the folded edge along the open edge making sure you catch the seam allowance on the inside.

STEP 2

Waistline elastic: Cut a piece of elastic the measurement of your waist plus 2cm (¾ in). Sew the elastic into a loop by overlapping the ends using the method described in the Tools and Techniques section. Mark the elastic into 2 equal points, and pin the elastic to the inside of the dress at the waistline, matching the marked points to the side seams. Using a wide zig zag stitch, sew the elastic to the fabric, stretching the elastic slightly as you sew.

TIPS AND OPTIONS

- USE LENGTHS OF RIBBON INSTEAD OF MAKING TIES FROM THE FABRIC FOR THE NECKLINE TIES.

Kaftan

A floaty kaftan is a quintessential summer garment. This design has a simple, v-neck shape that provides plenty of opportunity for adding trims and ribbon, and waistband ties or elastic to provide shape. This project has two variations, a short version and a maxi version.

MATERIALS AND EQUIPMENT

• Lightweight woven fabrics such as cotton and blends like poplin, batiste, lawn, gingham, or luxurious fabrics such as chiffon, georgette or beaded fabrics

• Narrow double fold bias binding for the short kaftan

• Narrow ribbon for the short kaftan

• Narrow elastic for the maxi kaftan

CUTTING OUT:

See templates section page 108–109 for patterns

The pattern template is the same for both short and long kaftans – cut the skirt portion at the marked lines for the short kaftan, for the long kaftan cut skirt to your ankles.

Cut out two pieces of the upper front, and one each of the lower front and the back along the folded edge as marked on the pattern.

Sewing Instructions: Short version:

STEP 1

Sew the shoulder seams: Sew the two front pieces to the back at the shoulder seam, with the right sides facing together. Neaten the raw edge of the seam, and press the seam allowance towards the back.

STEP 2

Finish the neckline edge: Finish the raw edges of the neckline and fold towards the inside 1cm (½ in). On the right side of the fabric stitch around the neck edge 1cm (½ in) from the folded edge, making sure you catch the seam allowance on the inside.

STEP 3

Join the front bodice and skirt: Sew the two front pieces of the bodice to the front skirt panel with the right sides of the fabric facing together, with the finished edges placed closely together at the centre front of the skirt panel. Finish the raw edge of the seam, and iron the seam allowance downwards.

STEP 4

Sew the side seams: With the right sides of the fabric facing together, sew the side seams from the sleeve edge to the bottom hem. Finish the raw edge and iron the seam flat open.

STEP 5

Waistband casing: On the right side of the fabric, sew the bias binding around the top placed just under the seam of the front and straight across the back. Leave a small gap at the centre front between the ends of the bias binding.

STEP 6

Insert ribbon: Stick a safety pin in one end of the ribbon and slide through one of the openings. Push the safety pin through the casing and out of the other opening. Pull the ribbon through so that there is an equal amount of ribbon hanging out of both ends and is long enough to tie together in a bow.

STEP 7

Sew the sleeve hems and bottom hem: Finish the raw edges of the sleeve hems and the bottom hem, and fold towards the inside by 1cm (½ in). On the outside sew around the sleeve hem and bottom hem, 1cm (½ in) from the folded edge, making sure you catch the seam allowance on the inside.

Maxi version:

Follow **Steps 1, 2** and **3** as described for the short version.

STEP 4

Sew the side seams: With the right sides of the fabric facing together, sew the side seams from the sleeve edge, stopping approximately 45cm (18 in) from the bottom edge of the dress (approximately at your knees), leaving the fabric open for a walking split. Neaten the raw edges, and press the seams flat open, including the open bottom half of the dress. On the right side of the fabric, sew from the hem up one side of the split, across the bottom of the end of the side seam and back down the other side to the hem again, catching the seam allowance on the inside. Do this on the other side too.

STEP 5

Elastic waistband: Cut a piece of elastic to a length that fits snugly around your rib cage plus 2cm (¾ in). Sew the elastic into a loop by overlapping the ends and sewing across the overlapped piece as described in the Tools and Techniques section. Mark this elastic into four equal quarter points with pins.

STEP 6

Pin the elastic to the inside of the top just under the seam line at the front piece, placing each of the four marked points with

the side seams, centre back and centre front. Using a zig zag stitch, sew the elastic to the fabric slightly stretching the elastic between the marked points as you sew.

TIPS AND OPTIONS

- DOUBLE FOLD BIAS BINDING IS A TYPE OF RIBBON THAT HAS THE RAW EDGES ALREADY FOLDED IN.

- TRY USING A DECORATIVE STITCH IF YOUR SEWING MACHINE HAS THEM, IN A CONTRASTING THREAD COLOUR TO TOPSTITCH AROUND THE NECKLINE EDGE, SLEEVE AND BOTTOM HEMS.

- SEW SOME DECORATIVE RIBBON AND TRIM AROUND THE NECKLINE EDGE, SLEEVE AND BOTTOM HEMS, LIKE THE TRIM USED ON THE MAXI DRESS.

- IF YOU HAVE AN OVERLOCKER, TRY DOING A NARROW ROLLED EDGE ALONG THE SLEEVE AND BOTTOM HEMS INSTEAD OF FOLDING UNDER AND TOPSTITCHING. THIS WILL CAUSE THE FABRIC TO RIPPLE, AND IS CALLED A 'LETTUCE EDGE'. CONSULT YOUR MANUAL TO SEE HOW TO DO THIS, AS THE SETTINGS WILL BE DIFFERENT FOR EACH TYPE OF MACHINE.

Kimono Jacket

A kimono jacket is a lightweight and flowing jacket that is perfect for covering up bare shoulders when those hot summer days turn into cooler evenings. Both sides of the fabric will show in this design, so try to choose fabrics where the wrong side looks as good as the right side.

MATERIALS AND EQUIPMENT:

Lightweight woven fabrics that drape well.

CUTTING OUT:

See templates section page 107 for pattern

Fold your fabric in half, and cut out the back pattern piece with the centre back along the folded edge of the fabric, and cut two pieces of the front pattern piece.

Sewing Instructions:

STEP 1

Sew the back neckline: Make a box pleat at the centre back neckline, by first marking the fold line and sewing lines on your fabric either using chalk or pins. Fold the fabric with the right sides facing at the marked fold line so that the marked sewing lines match up. Sew along the marked sewing lines from the neckline down 12cm (5 in). Iron the pleated fabric flat so that there is an equal amount of the pleat on either side of the stitched seam in the centre. Stitch across the top of the pleat close to the edge to hold it in place.

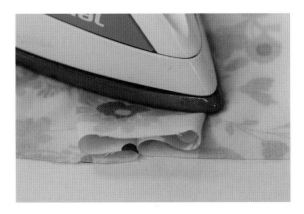

STEP 2

Sew the shoulder seams: Lay the front pieces on top of the back piece with the right sides of the fabric facing and sew along the shoulder seams 1cm (½ in) from the edge. Neaten the raw edge of the fabric and press the seam flat.

STEP 3

Sew the side seams: With the right sides of the fabric facing each other, sew along the side seams from the sleeve edge down to the bottom hem edge, 1cm (½ in) from the edge. Neaten the raw edge of the fabric and press the seam flat.

STEP 4

Finish the edges: Sew a narrow hem edge around the neckline, bottom hem and sleeve hems by folding the raw edge over by 0.5cm (¼ in) and press flat, and then fold over another 0.5cm (¼ in) and press flat so that the raw edge is fully enclosed. Sew close to the folded edge on the right side of the fabric all the way around the edge of the jacket and the sleeves, making sure you catch the seam allowance on the inside.

TIPS AND OPTIONS

- IF YOU DON'T LIKE THE LOOK OF A DIPPED HEM AT THE BACK OF THE KIMONO JACKET, CUT THE BOTTOM EDGE OF THE BACK PATTERN PIECE STRAIGHT ACROSS WHEN CUTTING THE PATTERN OUT FROM THE FABRIC.

Half Sarong

A short sarong is an extremely versatile garment, you can wear it as a skirt, a top, a mini dress or a scarf by draping and tying it in different ways. Use luxurious fabrics such as silk, chiffon or georgette for a glamorous look, or simple cotton fabrics for a poolside cover up.

MATERIALS AND EQUIPMENT

Lightweight woven fabrics such as cotton and blends like poplin, batiste, lawn, gingham, or silky fabrics such as chiffon, georgette or rayon.

CUTTING OUT

Cut out a rectangle of your fabric at least 1 and a half times your hip measurement, and as long as the distance from your waist to your knees.

Sewing Instructions

STEP 1

Sew the top edge: Make a narrow hem along one of the long edges of the rectangle by folding over the raw edge by 1cm (½ in) and press, and then fold over again by 1cm (½ in) and press flat. On the right side of the fabric and using a straight stitch sew 1cm (½ in) from the folded edge from one end of the rectangle to the other.

STEP 2

Fray the other edges: Using a pin, draw out threads from the edge of the fabric for a few centimetres around the three un-sewn edges.

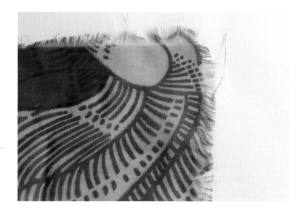

HALF SARONG

Full Length Sarong with Shoulder Straps

This full length sarong has shoulder straps so that you don't have to fiddle about with tying knots. To wear it, start by holding the fabric behind you with a strap in each hand, and wrap one side across your body and put a strap onto the opposite arm. Complete by wrapping the other side over the first layer and onto the opposite shoulder.

MATERIALS AND EQUIPMENT

Lightweight woven fabrics such as cotton and blends like poplin, batiste, lawn, gingham or a stretchy knit fabric such as jersey or interlock.

CUTTING OUT

Cut out a rectangle of fabric measuring 160cm (63 in) by 80cm (31½ in).

Cut two strips of fabric 40cm (15¾ in) by 4cm (1½ in) for the shoulder straps.

Sewing Instructions

STEP 1

Create the armholes: Cut a triangle from each end of the top edge, by measuring 15cm (6 in) across and down the edges from the corner.

STEP 2

Hem the edges: Sew a narrow hem the entire way around the edge of the sarong, by folding the raw edge over by 0.5cm (¼ in) and press flat, and then fold this edge over another 0.5cm (¼ in) and press flat so that the raw edge is fully enclosed. Sew close to the folded edge on the right side of the fabric all the way around the edge of the sarong, making sure you catch the seam allowance on the inside.

STEP 3

Sew the straps: Fold the two strips of fabric in half lengthways and sew 1cm (½ in) from the edge to create a long tube. Turn the tubes of fabric the right side out, following the method described in the Tools and Techniques section. Tuck the raw ends into the inside of the tube and press flat.

STEP 4

Attach the straps: Sew the ends of the strap to the sarong at either side of the diagonal line where you cut the triangle shape from the fabric.

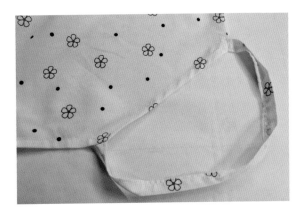

TIPS AND OPTIONS

- INSTEAD OF SEWING A NARROW HEM AROUND THE SIDES AND BOTTOM YOU COULD FRAY THESE EDGES, SIMILAR TO THE SHORT SARONG.

- MAKE THE SARONG AS LONG OR SHORT AS YOU LIKE.

Fabric Covered Beads

These beads are a great alternative to traditional jewellery for those days when you want to add some bling to your outfit but it's just too hot and sticky for anything. These are quick and simple and would make lovely gifts for your friends too.

MATERIALS AND EQUIPMENT

Lightweight woven fabrics such as cotton and blends or stretch knit fabrics such as jersey, interlock etc.

Large timber or plastic beads or marbles.

CUTTING OUT

Cut a length of fabric 1m (39 in) long, and as wide as the distance around the beads you are using plus 2cm (¾ in) for seam allowance

Sewing Instructions

STEP 1

Fold your fabric in half lengthways with the right sides facing together. Sew down the long edge 1cm (½ in) from the raw edge, using a straight stitch for a woven fabric or a stretch stitch for a knit fabric.

STEP 2

Turn the tube of fabric the right side out, using the method described in the Tools and Techniques section.

STEP 3

Tie a knot tightly at one end of the fabric tube 18cm (7 in) from one end.

STEP 4

Slide a bead into the tube and push it all the way to the knotted end. Tie another knot in the tube of fabric close to the bead.

STEP 5

Continue inserting beads and tying knots in the tube until it is as long as you would like it when draped around your neck. Cut off any excess fabric, leaving at least 18cm (7 in) of the tube after the last knot.

TIPS AND OPTIONS

INSTEAD OF TYING KNOTS IN BETWEEN THE BEADS YOU COULD TIE LITTLE BOWS USING THIN RIBBON IN A MATCHING OR CONTRASTING COLOUR. OR USE STRING OR THREAD WRAPPED AROUND THE TUBE A FEW TIMES AND KNOTTED TIGHTLY.

IF YOU ARE USING A STRETCHY FABRIC, YOU COULD TRY A VARIETY OF SIZES OF BEADS IN THE ONE NECKLACE. THIS WILL ONLY WORK ON STRETCH FABRIC HOWEVER TO ALLOW THE BEADS TO FIT IN THE TUBE.

INSTEAD OF TYING THE NECKLACE BEHIND YOUR NECK, YOU COULD SEW THE ENDS TOGETHER TO MAKE A LOOP – JUST MAKE SURE IT'S LONG ENOUGH TO SLIDE OVER YOUR HEAD.

MAKE A BRACELET IN THE SAME MANNER – IT WILL JUST REQUIRE A SHORTER LENGTH TUBE.

Bandana Headband

On hot and sticky days the best thing is to tie up your hair and keep it off your face with a headband. This bandana headband has a bit of a retro, 1950s housewife look about it that will look great when paired with a cool pair of sunglasses.

MATERIALS AND EQUIPMENT

Lightweight woven fabrics, such as cotton and cotton blend poplin, batiste, lawn, gingham etc.

Chopstick or pencil.

CUTTING OUT

Cut two rectangles 90cm (35½ in) long by 8cm (3⅛ in) wide. Cut the ends of the rectangles into a triangle shape, approximately 6cm (2⅜ in) from the end.

Sewing Instructions

STEP 1

Lay the two pieces of fabric together with the right sides facing and the cut edges aligned.

STEP 2

Start sewing in the middle of one of the long edges. Sew the entire way around the edge of the fabric 1cm (½ in) from the raw edge, stopping 5cm (2 in) from the point where you started sewing to leave a small opening in the seam.

STEP 3

Trim the fabric close to the sewing line at the pointy ends of the fabric.

STEP 4

Turn the bandana the right side out through the small opening in the middle of the long edge.

STEP 5

Using a chopstick or pencil, gently push out the pointy ends of the fabric.

STEP 6

Press the bandana flat, making sure that the raw edges of the small opening are folded to the inside.

STEP 7

Sew the small opening closed by hand-stitching with small stitches in a matching colour thread, or machine stitch the entire way around the bandana, stitching close to the edge.

TIPS AND OPTIONS

CUT OUT THE PATTERN PIECES FROM TWO DIFFERENT COLOURED FABRICS TO MAKE THE BANDANA REVERSIBLE – BOTH SIDES WILL SHOW WHEN TIED UP IN A KNOT.

SEW DIFFERENT TRIMS ONTO THE BANDANA, SUCH AS RIBBON OR RIC RAC AROUND THE EDGE OF THE BANDANA.

BANDANA HEADBAND

Shoulder Bag

During the summertime, a leather handbag seems too heavy and sticky to carry. This shoulder bag pattern made of fabric is far more comfortable to carry, and is the perfect size to carry the things you need for a shopping trip or a night out with friends. Choose bright fabrics to coordinate with your summer wardrobe.

MATERIALS AND EQUIPMENT:

• Heavy weight woven fabric for the bag body and straps for example cotton canvas, drill or denim

• Lightweight woven fabrics such as cotton and cotton blend poplin, batiste, lawn, gingham etc; or heavyweight woven fabric for the contrast flaps

• Elastic cord or a hair elastic

• Button

CUTTING OUT:

See templates section page 110 for pattern

Cut out one piece of the bag pattern in your main fabric. Trace the flap piece only to create a separate pattern piece, and cut out one piece of the flap pattern in your contrasting fabric. Cut two rectangular strips in either fabric 6cm (2⅜ in) by 70cm (27½ in) for the shoulder strap.

Sewing Instructions:

STEP 1

Sew the inside top edge: Neaten the raw edge of the top edge of the bag, and fold towards the wrong side of the fabric by 1cm (½ in). On the right side of the fabric sew the folded edge down, sewing 1cm (½ in) from the folded edge, making sure you catch the seam allowance on the inside.

STEP 2

Create the bottom of the bag: Fold the bag body along the line marked on the pattern, with the right sides of the fabric facing. The folded edge will form bottom of bag.

STEP 3

Sew the side seams: Pin the sides of the bag from the sewn edge of the top edge of the bag down to the folded edge of the bottom of the bag, sewing 1cm (½ in) from the raw edge of the fabric. At the point you started sewing, make a small cut in the seam allowance from the raw edge to the sewing line.

STEP 4

Sew the contrasting flap: Turn the bag over so that the sewn top edge of the bag is facing down and the long edge of the bag is facing up. Pin the flap piece to the rounded top edge of the bag, with right sides of the fabric facing and the straight edge folded to the wrong side of the fabric by 1cm (½ in).

STEP 5

At the centre of the flap, slide a loop of elastic cord or a hair elastic in between the layers of fabric and pin in place.

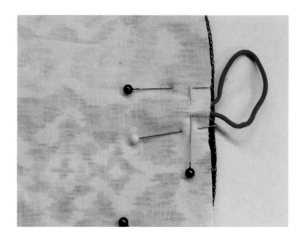

STEP 6

Sew around the flap edge, 1cm (½ in) from the raw edge, starting and finishing at the small cuts you made in Step 3. Make sure you backstitch over the elastic to make sure it is securely attached, and trim the excess elastic away.

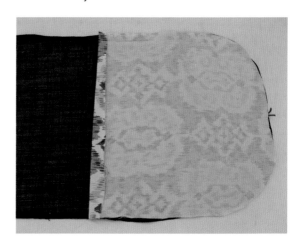

SHOULDER BAG

STEP 7

Turn the flap section the right way out, and press the flap flat at the edges. On the right side of the fabric, sew the straight edge of the contrast flap piece to the bag.

STEP 8

Finish the body of the bag: Turn the body of the bag the right way out, and push the corners out gently with a chopstick or pencil. Handsew a button to the centre front close to the bottom edge, making sure you only sew through the outer layer.

STEP 9

Make the shoulder straps: Pin the two rectangle strips of fabric together with the right sides facing and sew down both long edges 1cm (½ in) from the raw edge to create a long tube. Turn the fabric tube the right way out and press flat. Tuck the raw ends inside the tube and press flat.

STEP 10

Stitch three evenly spaced lines along the shoulder strap to give the strap some structure.

STEP 11

Attach the shoulder strap: Sew the strap to the sides of the bag near the top edge of the bag, evenly spaced on either side of the side seam.

TIPS AND OPTIONS

TRY USING DIFFERENT MATERIALS FOR THE SHOULDER STRAP FOR A DIFFERENT LOOK:

FOR A FAUX FRENCH BAG LOOK TRY A THIN METAL CHAIN PURCHASED FROM THE FABRIC STORE OR HARDWARE STORE. HAND SEW THE END OF THE CHAIN TO THE SIDES OF THE BAG.

FOR AN EARTHY LOOK, AN OLD LEATHER BELT WITH THE BUCKLE CUT OFF WOULD LOOK GREAT. SEW THE BOTTOM OF THE STRAPS TO THE SIDES OF THE BAG WITH A STRONGER MACHINE NEEDLE TO GET THROUGH THE THICKER FABRIC.

FOR A VINTAGE LOOK USE A SCARF, FOLDED INTO A NARROW TUBE OF FABRIC AND TIED INTO A KNOT IN THE CENTRE TO KEEP THE TUBE SHAPE. MACHINE SEW ACROSS THE ENDS OF THE SCARF A FEW TIMES TO MAKE SURE THE SCARF IS SECURELY ATTACHED TO THE SIDES OF THE BAG. SECOND HAND STORES HAVE LOTS OF CHEAP COLOURFUL SCARVES FOR SALE AND ARE PERFECT FOR UP CYCLING INTO A NEW USE LIKE THIS.

Beach Bag

This bag is big enough to carry all of the essentials you need when going to the beach or sitting beside the pool such as a beach towel and magazines, and the outer pocket will keep your phone and sunglasses in easy reach. And if your bottle of sunscreen leaks inside you can easily throw this bag in the washing machine and it will look as good as new.

MATERIALS

Sturdy, heavy weight woven fabric for example cotton canvas, drill or denim.

CUTTING OUT

• Cut a rectangle of fabric 52cm (20½ in) wide by 92cm (36¼ in) long for the body of the bag.

• Cut two rectangles of fabric 65cm (25½ in) by 10cm (4 in) for the straps.

• Cut one rectangle of fabric 23cm (9 in) by 15cm (6 in) for the pocket.

Sewing Instructions

STEP 1

To make the bag body: Fold the fabric in half lengthways with the right sides of the fabric facing each other. Sew both sides of the fabric from the folded edge to the top of the bag. Turn the bag right side out and press the side seams flat.

STEP 2

Sew the top edge: Fold 1.5cm (½ in) of the top edge of the bag towards the wrong side of the fabric and press flat. Then fold this down another 1.5cm (½ in) and press flat to form a hem around the top edge of the bag with the raw edge enclosed. On the right side of the fabric stitch around the top of the bag 1.5cm (½ in) from the folded edge, making sure you catch the seam allowance on the inside.

STEP 3

To make the pocket: Fold all the raw edges of the rectangle towards the wrong side of the fabric by 1cm (½ in), and press flat. On the right side of the fabric, sew across one of the long edges of the rectangle 1cm (½ in) from the folded edge to create the top edge of the pocket.

STEP 4

Sew the pocket to the bag: Pin the pocket to the centre of one side of the bag, on the right side of the fabric with the sewn edge at the top. Stitch around the side and bottom edge of the pocket using a straight edge, close to the edge of the pocket. Backstitch at the start and the end of sewing the pocket to the bag to reinforce the top edges.

STEP 5

To make the straps: Fold the long strips of fabric in half lengthways with the right sides of the fabric facing each other. Sew down the long edge of the rectangle 1cm (½ in) from the raw edge to create a fabric tube. Backstitch at the start and finish off sewing the seam so that it doesn't come undone when turning the tubes of fabric right side out.

STEP 6

Turn the tubes right side out following the method in the Tools and Techniques section to create the shoulder straps. Fold the raw ends of the straps to the inside by 1cm (½ in) and press flat.

STEP 7

Attach the straps: Sew one strap to each side of the bag. Pin the ends of the strap 10cm (4 in) from the side seams and sew the bottom 3cm (1¼ in) of the strap to the top edge of the bag by sewing a square with a cross in the middle of the square at the end of the strap.

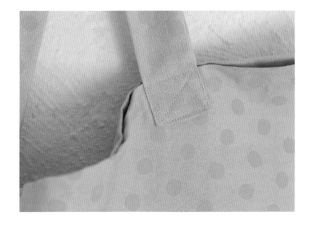

TIPS AND OPTIONS

- YOU COULD USE DIFFERENT MATERIALS FOR THE STRAPS SUCH AS LEATHER OR CANVAS STRAPS BOUGHT FROM FABRIC AND CRAFT STORES, OR EVEN RECYCLE OLD BELTS TO MAKE THIS AN EVEN QUICKER PROJECT TO SEW.

- MAKE THE POCKET FROM A DIFFERENT COLOURED FABRIC SO THAT IT STANDS OUT AGAINST THE FABRIC OF THE BAG.

Sunhat

A sunhat is a summer essential when the sun is bearing down. This hat has a medium sized brim, which is wide enough to keep the sun off your face but not too wide that it flops down in your face or blows away in the wind.

MATERIALS AND EQUIPMENT

Mid to heavy weight woven fabric such as cotton canvas, drill or denim.

CUTTING OUT

See templates section page 111 for pattern

Cut out six of the triangle shaped crown pattern pieces.

Cut out two of the brim pieces, with the wider straight edge on the fold of the fabric as indicated on the pattern.

Sewing Instructions

STEP 1

Sew the crown: Sew the triangle shaped pieces together in pairs, 1cm (½ in) from the edge and starting at the dot marked on the pattern. Press the sewn seams flat open. Then sew the pairs of triangles together, until the crown is all joined together in a circle. Press all the sewn seams flat open.

STEP 2

Sew the brim: For each brim piece, sew the narrow straight edge together with the right sides of the fabric facing each other 1cm (½ in) from the edge, to create a circular piece. Press the sewn seams flat open.

STEP 3

Pin one brim piece to the other, with right sides of the fabric facing each other and the sewn seams lined up. Sew around the outside edge of the brim 1cm (½ in) from the cut edge.

STEP 4

Make small cuts in the seam allowance from the raw edge to near the sewn line, the entire way around the brim edge to help the curved seam sit flat when turned the right way out.

STEP 5

Turn the brim the right side out, and press the sewn edges flat.

STEP 6

Joining the brim and the crown: With the right sides together, pin one layer of the brim at the inner edge to the bottom edge of the crown. Sew completely around the circle 1cm (½ in) from the raw edges.

STEP 7

Press the seams away from the inside of the hat towards the brim. Turn under 1cm (½ in) of the raw edge of the free layer of brim fabric that is on the inside of the brim. Press this turned under edge flat and pin to the hat, close to the sewn seam, so that the raw edges are enclosed. Hand stitch this seam closed, or machine stitch around the brim close to the edge of this seam.

STEP 8

Topstitch the brim: For decoration and to stiffen the brim, sew around the brim starting from the outside edge of the brim. Use the edge of the presser foot to make sure the lines are evenly spaced.

TIPS AND OPTIONS

- USE CONTRASTING THREAD FOR THE DECORATIVE STITCHING ON THE BRIM TO MAKE IT REALLY STAND OUT, OR USE MATCHING THREAD FOR A SUBTLE LOOK. INSTEAD OF USING A STRAIGHT STITCH, TRY A DECORATIVE STITCH IF YOUR SEWING MACHINE HAS THEM.

- IF YOU DON'T WANT TO SEW THE DECORATIVE STITCHING ON THE BRIM, APPLY SOME IRON ON INTERFACING TO THE INSIDE OF ONE OF THE BRIM PIECES. THIS WILL GIVE THE BRIM STIFFNESS.

- YOU COULD USE A NUMBER OF DIFFERENT COLOURED FABRICS TO MAKE THE BRIM AND THE CROWN OF THE HAT.

- TO MAKE THE BRIM WIDER, ADD SOME EXTRA WIDTH AT THE OUTSIDE EDGE OF THE BRIM PATTERN PIECE – DON'T CHANGE THE INNER EDGE OF THE BRIM PATTERN PIECE OTHERWISE IT WON'T BE THE SAME SIZE AS THE CROWN.

Pattern Templates

WRAP SKIRT

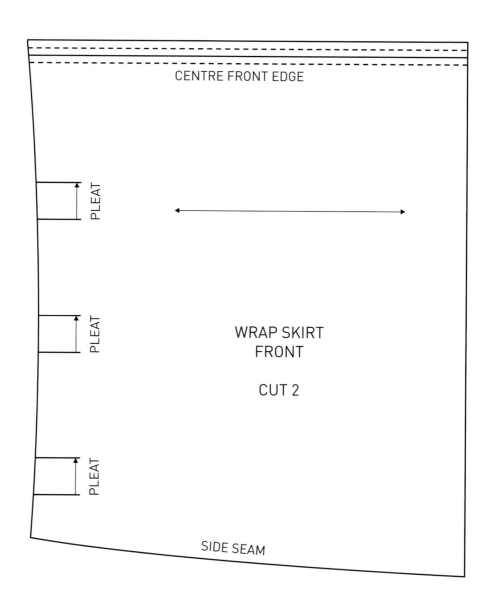

CENTRE FRONT EDGE

PLEAT

PLEAT

PLEAT

WRAP SKIRT
FRONT

CUT 2

SIDE SEAM

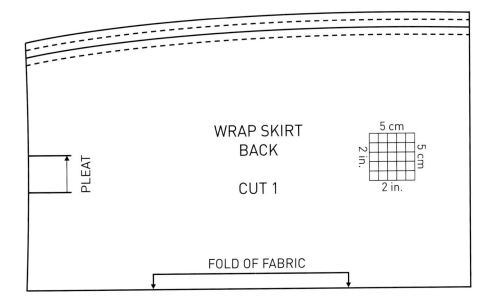

WRAP SKIRT
BACK

CUT 1

PLEAT

5 cm
5 cm
2 in.
2 in.

FOLD OF FABRIC

PENCIL SKIRT

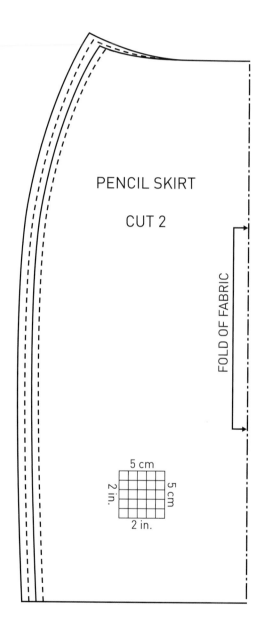

PENCIL SKIRT

CUT 2

FOLD OF FABRIC

5 cm

5 cm

2 in.

2 in.

PANTS POCKET TECHNIQUE

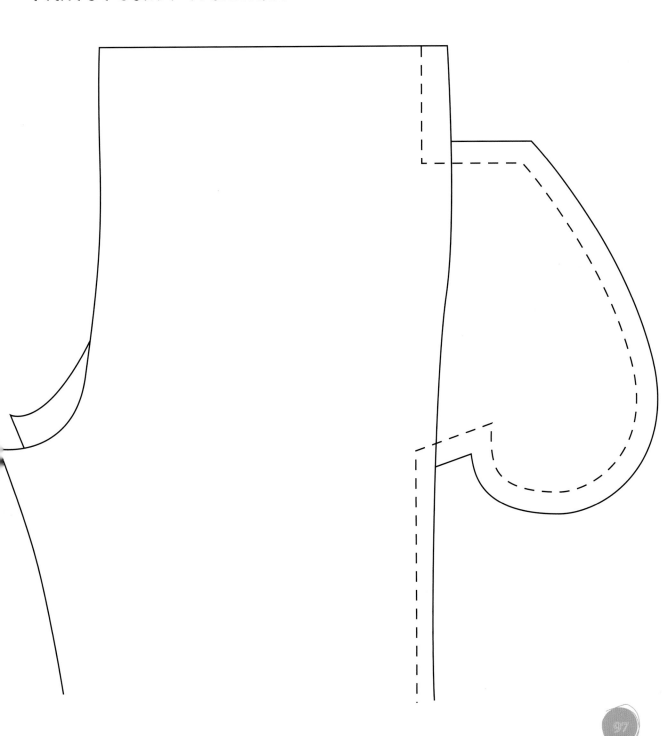

SINGLET TOP/DRESS

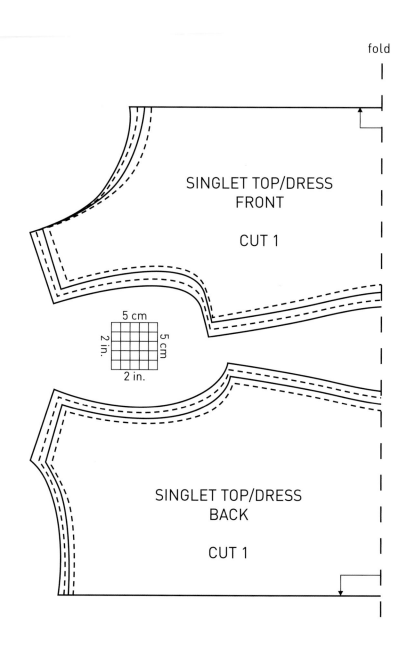

fold

SINGLET TOP/DRESS
FRONT

CUT 1

5 cm

2 in.

5 cm

2 in.

SINGLET TOP/DRESS
BACK

CUT 1

fold

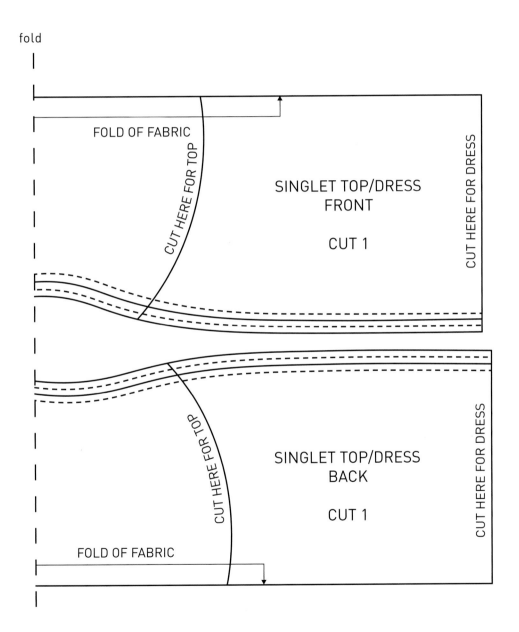

FOLD OF FABRIC

CUT HERE FOR TOP

SINGLET TOP/DRESS
FRONT

CUT 1

CUT HERE FOR DRESS

CUT HERE FOR TOP

SINGLET TOP/DRESS
BACK

CUT 1

CUT HERE FOR DRESS

FOLD OF FABRIC

DRAWSTRING PANTS

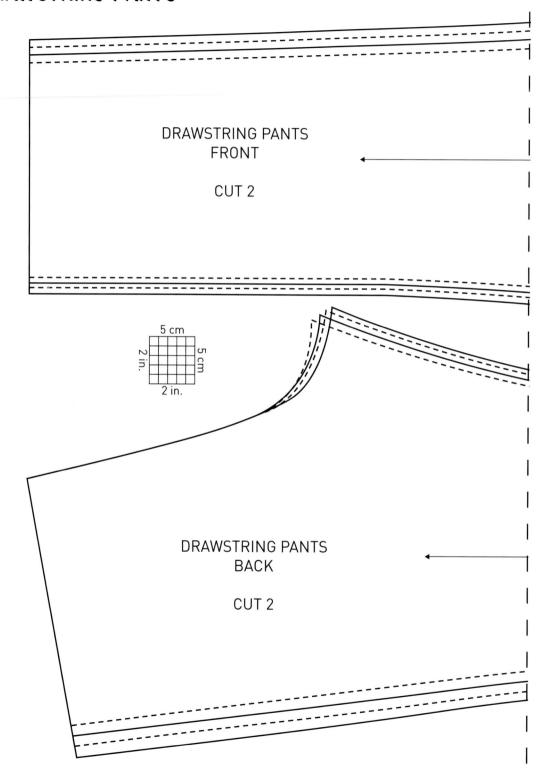

DRAWSTRING PANTS
FRONT

CUT 2

5 cm
2 in.
5 cm
2 in.

DRAWSTRING PANTS
BACK

CUT 2

fold

DRAWSTRING PANTS
FRONT

CUT 2

DRAWSTRING PANTS
BACK

CUT 2

SIMPLE SHORTS/PANTS

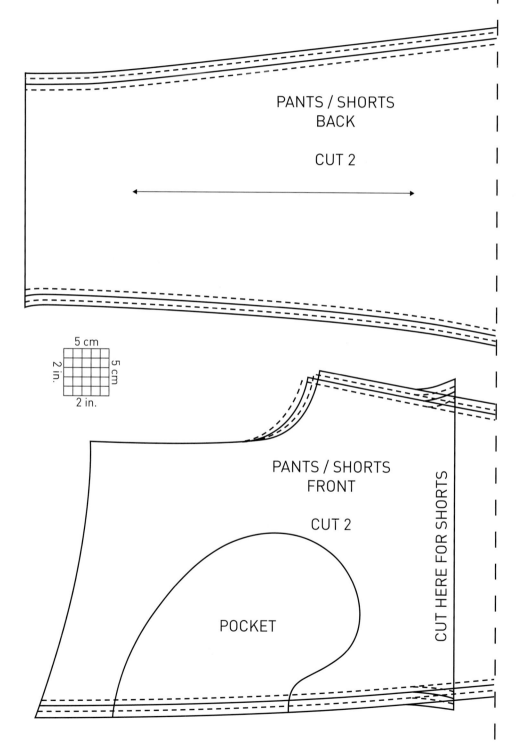

PANTS / SHORTS
BACK

CUT 2

5 cm

2 in.

5 cm

2 in.

PANTS / SHORTS
FRONT

CUT 2

CUT HERE FOR SHORTS

POCKET

fold

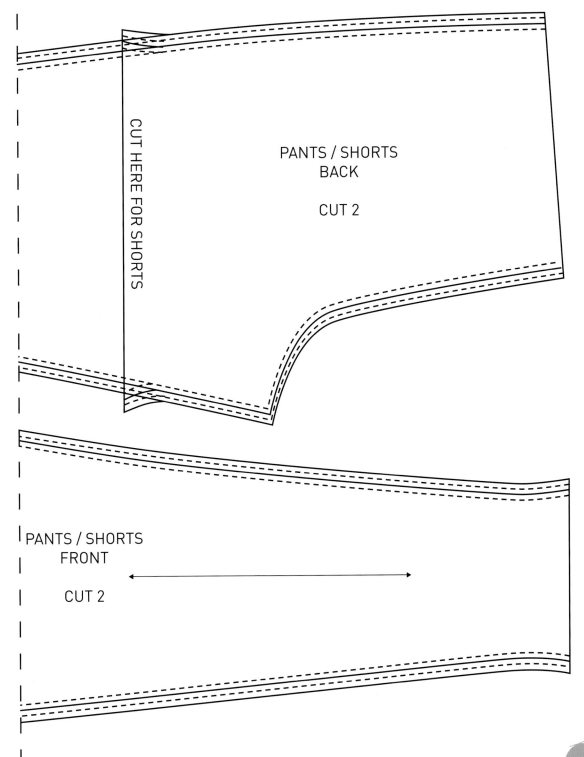

CUT HERE FOR SHORTS

PANTS / SHORTS
BACK

CUT 2

PANTS / SHORTS
FRONT

CUT 2

DRAPE NECK TOP/DRESS

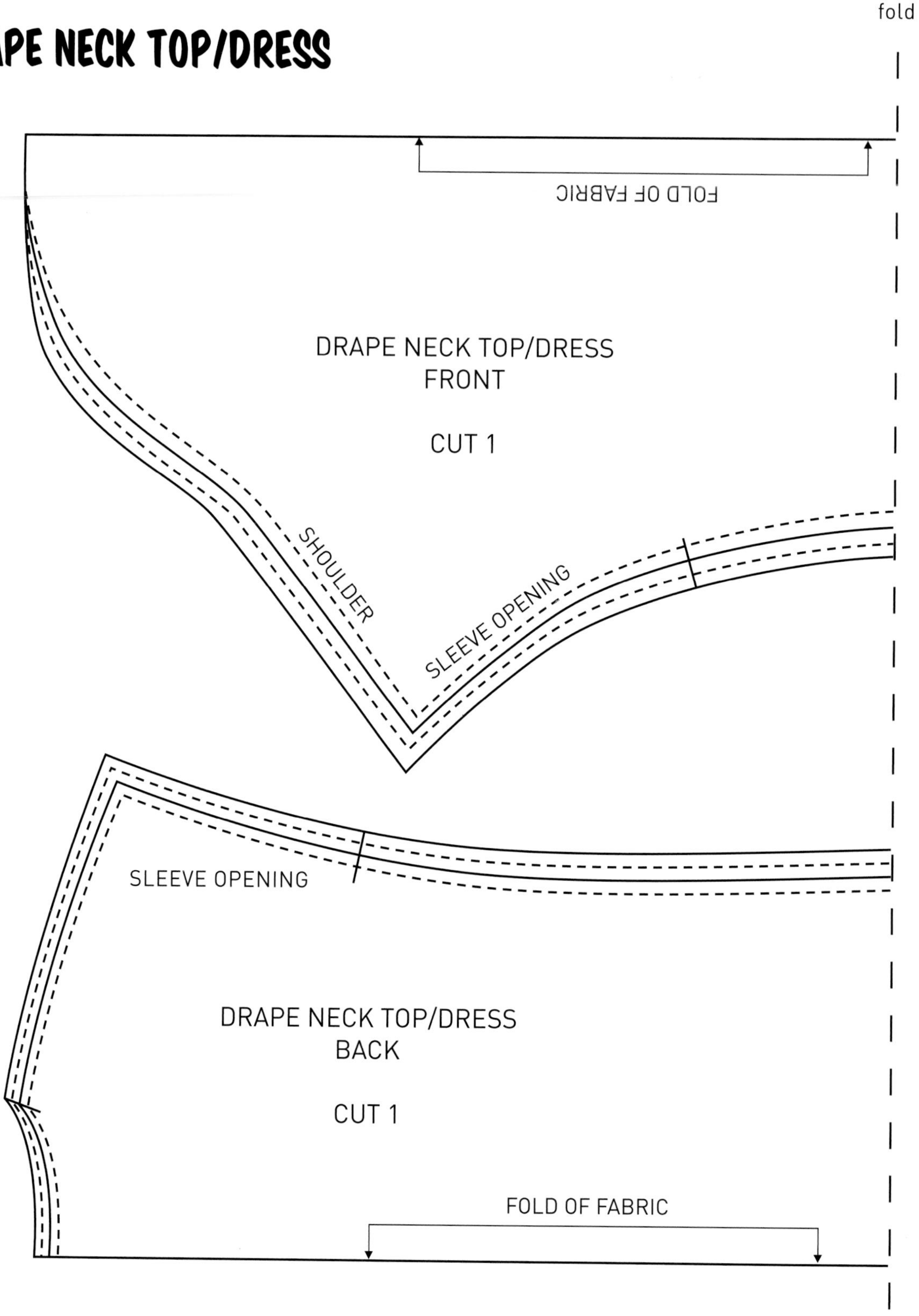

fold
FOLD OF FABRIC
DRAPE NECK TOP/DRESS
FRONT
CUT 1
SHOULDER
SLEEVE OPENING
SLEEVE OPENING
DRAPE NECK TOP/DRESS
BACK
CUT 1
FOLD OF FABRIC

fold

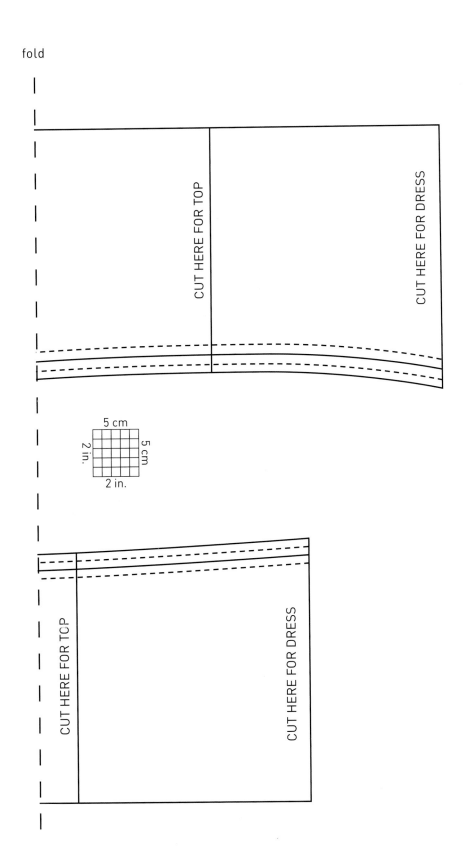

CUT HERE FOR TOP

CUT HERE FOR DRESS

5 cm

2 in.

5 cm

2 in.

CUT HERE FOR TOP

CUT HERE FOR DRESS

HALTER NECK DRESS/MAXI

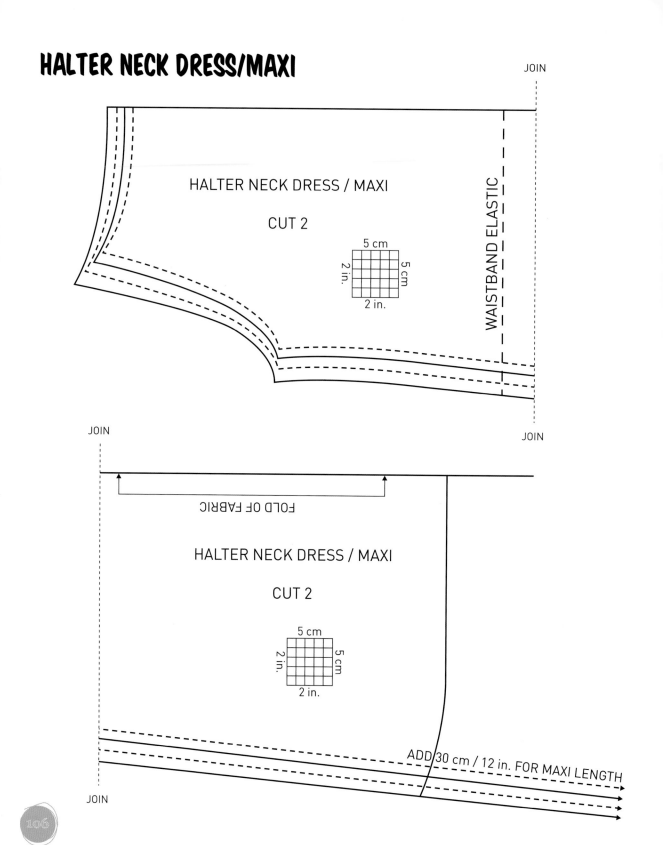

KIMONO

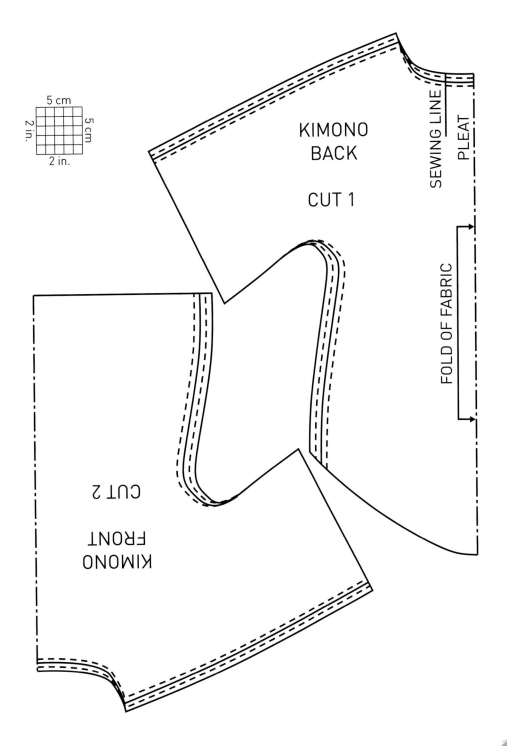

5 cm

2 in.

5 cm

2 in.

KIMONO
BACK

CUT 1

SEWING LINE

PLEAT

FOLD OF FABRIC

KIMONO
FRONT

CUT 2

KAFTAN

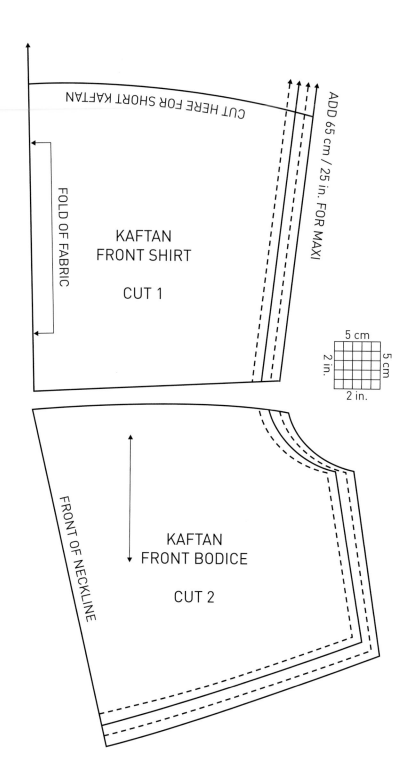

CUT HERE FOR SHORT KAFTAN

ADD 65 cm / 25 in. FOR MAXI

FOLD OF FABRIC

KAFTAN
FRONT SHIRT

CUT 1

5 cm

2 in.

5 cm

2 in.

FRONT OF NECKLINE

KAFTAN
FRONT BODICE

CUT 2

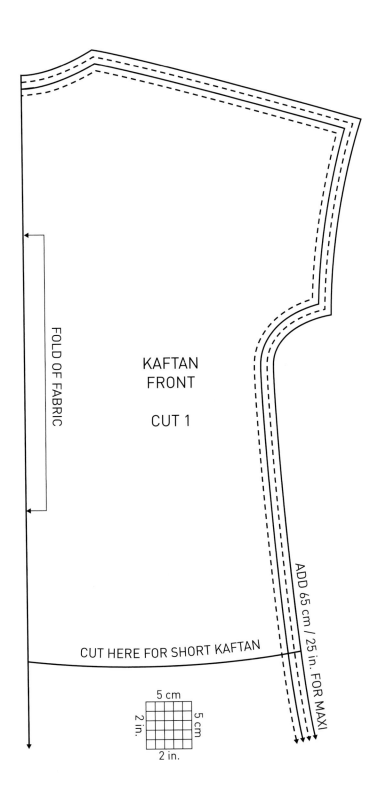

FOLD OF FABRIC

KAFTAN
FRONT

CUT 1

ADD 65 cm / 25 in. FOR MAXI

CUT HERE FOR SHORT KAFTAN

5 cm

2 in.

5 cm

2 in.

SHOULDER BAG

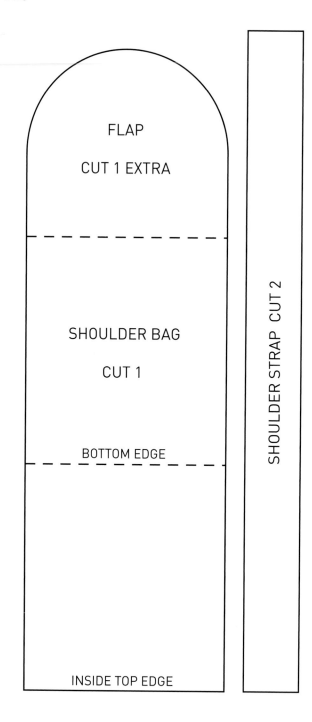

FLAP

CUT 1 EXTRA

SHOULDER BAG

CUT 1

BOTTOM EDGE

INSIDE TOP EDGE

SHOULDER STRAP CUT 2

5 cm

2 in.

5 cm

2 in.

SUN HAT

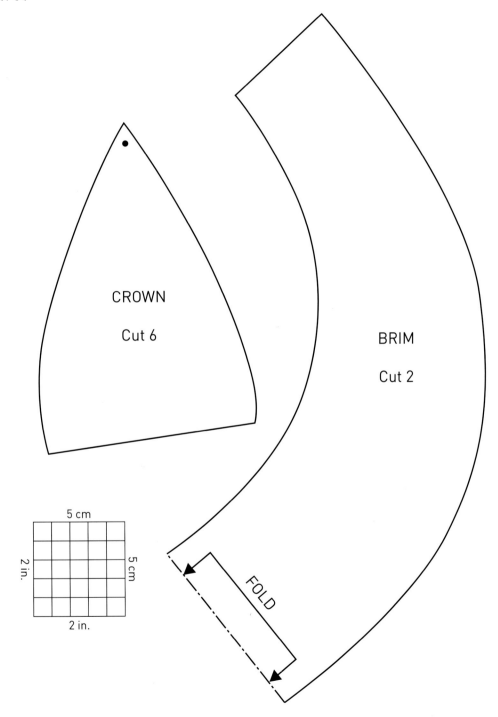

CROWN

Cut 6

BRIM

Cut 2

5 cm

5 cm

2 in.

2 in.

FOLD